A guide for
millennial women
to speaking and
being heard

SHE
SAID

PATRICIA SEABRIGHT

She Said!

First published in 2020 by

Panoma Press Ltd
48 St Vincent Drive, St Albans, Herts, AL1 5SJ, UK
info@panomapress.com
www.panomapress.com

Book layout by Neil Coe.

978-1-784529-24-6

The right of Patricia Seabright to be identified as the author of this work has been asserted in accordance with sections 77 and 78 of the Copyright, Designs and Patents Act 1988.

A CIP catalogue record for this book is available from the British Library.

This book is available online and in bookstores.

Dedication

To my Mother, who always encouraged me to speak up;
to my husband, who has supported that outspokenness
for the last 30 years; and to my daughters, who are
growing into articulate young women who will certainly
be heard in the world.

Acknowledgements

This book builds on firm foundations. It is the culmination of my 30 years in business and working with people and businesses across many industries and countries. It comes from working specifically on communication, influence and persuasion with hundreds of groups and thousands of women.

It is the result of my research, which hugely benefited from the work of many great female role models who have written books to share their wisdom, women like Sheryl Sandberg, Carrie Gracie, Helen Lewis and Caroline Criado-Perez.

And it also comes from interviews I have done with a range of amazing and fantastic women who generously shared their time, enthusiasm and experiences. They are:

- The Rt Reverend Anne Hollinghurst, Bishop of Aston

- Annetta Hewko, consultant, former European general manager, consumer goods industry

- Dr Arinola Araba, entrepreneur, educator and author

- Clare McLean, communications director, data analytics industry

- Deborah Mackiewicz, consultant and senior

manager in the consumer goods industry

- Emily Hunt, author and data storyteller

- Hayley Everett, multimedia reporter, publishing industry

- Janet Morris, NED, former sales director of Cambridge International Exams

- Juliet Archer-Reeves, principal project manager, engineering industry

- Jemma Harrison, technology director, financial services

- Lisa McCurdy, sales and marketing director, pharmaceutical industry

- Lucy Vernall, general counsel and chief people officer, fintech industry (GC of the year 2019)

- Martine Croxall, BBC news presenter and NUJ representative

- Reverend Jos Perris, school chaplain, former managing director, advertising industry

- Margaret Chapman, head teacher, state girls' school

- Miriam Reid, executive manager, insurance industry

- Reem Zahran, chief operating officer, financial services industry

- Ruth Dearnley, OBE, CEO, anti-human trafficking charity

- Sara Britcliffe, member of parliament

- Seema Kennedy, former member of parliament, minister and parliamentary private secretary to Theresa May

- Sylvia Evans, global head of communications, financial services industry

- Sally Bishop, actress, drama teacher and voice coach

- Sophie Jenkins, sales executive and apprentice

- Theo Clark, member of parliament

- Vasudha Bajaj, product manager, pharmaceutical industry

- Vanessa Dal Busco, marketing and tech evangelist

- Wendy Greig-Ewens, global technology director, financial services

- Zoe Amar, founder of Zoe Amar Digital, chair of Charity Digital Code

- Zoe Hancock, principal, FE College

Contents

Introduction: The challenges for women

The ability to speak, speak up, speak out and be heard matters.

On a micro level, it matters to personal success and on a macro level, it matters to the issue of gender equality. Sheryl Sandberg's excellent book *Lean In: Women, Work and the Will to Lead*, was a game changer. However, it is one thing to say women must lean in, take a seat at the table and be proactive in speaking up, but the million dollar question is often, HOW?

How do you speak up without being accused of being 'bossy, screechy or unfeminine'? How do you make your point heard without being dismissed as 'unlikeable' or without getting hammered as a 'feminazi'? How do you remain determined and focused without being dismissed as a 'difficult woman'?

The facts are that women speak less and are heard less than men. Too often when women do not feel heard, we brush it aside, we blame it on other factors, other people, character shortcomings, or just the way of the world. We do not often have the opportunity to step back and recognise what is really going on. This is an issue because it stops us from developing strategies to address what is happening.

We tell ourselves it should not matter, that it shouldn't hurt or anger us, that it is not significant or limiting.

I worked in business-to-business sales in the corporate world for 15 years and eventually left to start my own business. I had concluded that I just was not getting on as well as I wanted to and not enjoying it. I thought at the time I was just too independent and not a very good 'corporate citizen'. Looking back with the benefit of hindsight, I realise that, in fact, I was simply not navigating well the unconscious bias that was baked into the corporate world I inhabited. So, this book is about how you might read things differently, which will enable you to shift your thinking and feelings to respond more constructively.

Aims of the book

This book aims to help individual millennial women achieve their goals. It is designed to help them better understand the subtle, subconscious pressures that sometimes makes them feel unwilling to speak up or like they're banging their heads against a brick (or maybe glass?) wall when they do.

This book is about ensuring that this generation does not fight the same battles as the previous ones. It is about making practical adaptations necessary to both succeed on a personal level and advocate for some of the systemic, structural changes that are needed. It is about giving women practical tools and techniques to enable and support them in speaking up, speaking out and being heard. It is about empowering millennial women to fast forward their progress.

In all the chapters there will be two parts:

1. Discussion of the topic itself

2. Discussion of what to do about it, offering practical tactics and techniques. Within that there is a natural split giving you two different options for how to operate:

   a. how to navigate the issue

   b. how to challenge the issue

Each woman and each situation are different and one size does not fit all. What this approach does is give you choices and options on what is the best way for you to proceed.

Part 1 – AWARENESS

This section looks at raising women's awareness: if you do not like to speak out, why is that? What are the subtle (and sometimes not so subtle) factors at play that make you feel uncomfortable and less inclined to speak? Understanding where some of our thoughts and feelings on the subject of speaking come from is the first step towards creating a platform that enables us to better advocate for ourselves. Within that I'll look at:

- **Chapter 1 – Why speaking matters:** why speaking (in meetings, making speeches and giving presentations) matters for you and your career and is such a disproportionately important skill

- **Chapter 2 – The 4,000-year silence project:** the historical context and why women's voices have been suppressed throughout history

- **Chapter 3 – The princess and the imposter:** why girls in our society are raised to be perfect princesses (and it's not just Disney's fault!) and trying to live up to the perfection ideal creates constant tension and feelings of inadequacy

- **Chapter 4 – The Likeability Paradox:** why it is that professional women can be liked or respected, but being both is tough – maybe even impossible – and what to do about it

- **Chapter 5 – The critic and the troll:** why women are subject to more criticism and judgment than men; why the nature of that criticism is often more personal and how this works to keep women silent

Part 2 – SKILL

Once you have got your mind in the right place to speak out, how do you execute? You may have dealt with some of the psychological barriers to speaking but what next? How do you deal with some of the skills and practicalities of speaking, particularly as relevant to women? I have interviewed dozens of women from all types of organisations and a wide range of industries and sectors, including the media, church and politics. Their wisdom and experience have been rolled into this section.

In Part 2 I'll cover:

- **Chapter 6 – Language:** the language women use to undermine themselves and better alternatives

- **Chapter 7 – Vocal quality:** some common pitfalls for women and how to avoid them (how you sound is key to communication)

- **Chapter 8 – Body language:** techniques to ensure that you come across confidently and powerfully (50% of your message comes across from your body language)

- **Chapter 9 – Emotion and empathy:** why emotion can a double-edged sword for women's communication and the skilled balancing act of how to harness women's strengths in emotional intelligence without being seen as 'weak' or 'soft'

- **Chapter 10 – Behavioural style:** how your individual personality and behavioural style makes you more or less susceptible to some of the challenges of speaking as a female

Part 3 – APPLICATION / ACTION

In this section, you will find:

- **Chapter 11 – Meetings:** a summary and combination of the practical approaches discussed, along with a checklist of 10 key things to consider when preparing for meetings

- **Chapter 12 – Presentations and Speeches:** a checklist of 10 key things to consider when preparing for and delivering presentations or speeches

This book is meant to be a handbook. Its purpose is to raise millennial women's awareness of the subtle but insidious issues that prevent women from speaking publicly and being fully heard. It is designed to offer practical techniques and approaches to help women, particularly women in the earlier phases of their lives and careers, to be heard and achieve their goals. I am keen to engage with you and hear your stories, you can get in touch with me at www.patriciaseabright.com and www.archimedesspeaks.com

PART 1

AWARENESS

Part 1 deals with understanding and recognising some of
the social norms, stereotypes, and paradigms that affect
women and their willingness to speak and their ability to
be heard.

CHAPTER 1

Why speaking matters

Why does speaking matter to individual women?

It does not matter whether you are speaking one-to-one or in a meeting, a presentation or a speech. For you to make an impact and advocate for yourself, your ideas, or your beliefs, to get what you want and need, you must speak to influence. It could be speaking to your boss to ask for a pay rise. It could be speaking in a PTA meeting to influence the right decisions for your child's school. It could be making a presentation to win a million-pound contract, or it could be speaking in Parliament on an issue that changes the course of history. Whatever the occasion, it is a disproportionately important skill. It matters at all levels.

History is littered with examples of speeches that made a crucial difference. A good speech or public debate resulted in Kennedy's victory over Nixon in 1960 and David Cameron beating David Davis (the huge favourite) to the Conservative Party leadership in 2005. It is why, in the 1940s, Lord Halifax failed to persuade Parliament to capitulate and make peace with Hitler, and Churchill succeeded in persuading them to fight on.

Steve Jobs' speeches are arguably why Apple attracts almost a cult following from its customers with commensurate loyalty to their premium-priced products. Throughout history, of course, we've heard more about men's speeches, but women too have a proud history of pivotally important speeches, from Queen Elizabeth I inspiring the English troops at Tilbury to fight against the Armada in 1588 to Malala Yousafzai rallying world leaders to the cause of girls' education at her speech at the UN in 2013, or Greta Thunberg's passionate and urgent speeches on climate change.

More recently, in the protests and unrest that broke out in the US and around the world in the wake of the killing of George Floyd (by a white police officer kneeling on his neck) in 2020, we saw numerous examples of powerful, impromptu speeches on the streets from protestors and police officers alike imploring people to protest peacefully. Many of these speeches were incredibly effective in reducing violence in the moment and ensuring that the main message of the Black Lives Matter protests was heard.

What makes speaking in public critical is that it is your shop front: it is the basis on which most people judge others. When you get to be reasonably senior in any walk of life, the majority of the people in your organisation do not see much of you day to day, only your closest team do. So, they judge you on your reputation, and much of that comes from what they see and hear of you in public forums such as meetings and company or team events and presentations. If you have political aspirations, your actual or potential constituents will mainly know you from your speeches (live or on social media).

I once coached a CEO and a sales VP at an all-company event at a large venue in London with an audience of several thousands. They both gave great speeches. I did not coach the marketing VP. He got up to speak and sadly did a really bad job. He had attractive visual slides but they didn't seem to relate to anything he was talking about, the flow of the presentation wasn't easy to follow and then, he dropped his notes. What followed was 10 minutes (OK, that's an exaggeration, it was perhaps a minute) while he scrabbled around on the floor trying to gather them up and reorder them before he continued.

Because I had coached the CEO and sales VP, I had access to the subsequent event feedback. The comments on his speech were not, 'Oh dear what a poor public speaker!', but rather 'What's an idiot like this doing as our marketing VP?' This was very unfair in many respects: this individual was a very strong marketing VP, but most people in his organisation didn't know that. Most did not see and hear from him that much on a day-to-day basis, so their opinion of him necessarily hinged on what they saw of him when he spoke at events.

A Catalyst (catalyst.org) study[1] found that self-advocacy skills – the ability to speak up for yourself – has a higher correlation to workplace status and pay than merit. In other words, it may not be fair, but it is true: ***speaking well is better for your career than working hard***. This is particularly relevant for millennials, many of whom have grown up more used to communicating using text and emoji than the more formal structure of meetings and presentations.

Speaking up and speaking out has however proved a tricky area for women

Amy Giddon, who was head of women's leadership development at Barnard College in New York, did some research that concluded: 'There is a disconnect between women's confidence in their skills and abilities (which is often high) and their confidence in their ability to navigate the system to achieve the recognition and advancement they feel they deserve. Self-advocacy is a big part of this, and it is identified by many women in the study as the biggest barrier to their advancement.'[2] Women do not lack expertise, knowledge, potential or inner confidence; what they often struggle with is the ability to comfortably speak well about that knowledge, expertise or potential.

I have spent 30 years in business and worked with large numbers of highly competent, very impressive women. Sadly, a common theme has been that so many of these women have often struggled to be willing and able to speak up and speak out at public and internal events and meetings. I've identified a consistent pattern of women finding ways to avoid speaking engagements, ranging from simply not volunteering to speak to coming up with a creative array of good reasons to delegate that task to junior colleagues. I come across women who are technically brilliant but feel tongue-tied and incapable of speaking up even when they really need to.

When I ask why, they often say they perceive themselves to be bad at it or just don't like it. Many report feeling terrified by having to speak in public. One woman I coached, who was a director in a public sector organisation, was so scared that she needed to take beta blockers to slow her heart rate every time she had to make a presentation. Frequently, however, the women I've spoken to just aren't really clear on why they don't like it. It is just deeply ingrained, largely subconscious, societal conditioning that makes them very adamant that they prefer not to speak.

Some women don't dislike it, some even say they do enjoy it, but even they still encounter difficulties when speaking up and, critically, struggle to be 'heard'. I have frequently been told that when women do speak up, they are often ignored or interrupted, or both. Carrie Gracie, in talking about her struggle for equal pay in the BBC, described the environment as 'fighting in a workplace in which women's ideas were often marginalised, ignored or credited to men'. One millennial female MP recently told me she felt she had had to 'fight my whole life to be heard'.

Women's voices being ignored is well documented in numerous studies. For example, research from George Washington University found that men interrupted women 33% more often than they interrupted other men.[3] Women's points are also often ignored until they are taken up by a man and restated as his thoughts. US Supreme

Court Justice Ruth Bader Ginsberg has often spoken about her experiences of this.

This appropriation of ideas by men (or 'bropropriation'!) is not new. The 1988 cartoon below, 'Thank you, Miss Triggs', by Riana Duncan illustrates this point, which remains true today.[4] Almost all of the senior women I interviewed for this book had examples of how this has happened to them and, in many cases, still happens frequently.

"That's an excellent suggestion, Miss Triggs. Perhaps one of the men here would like to make it."

And this matters. A lot.

Every time a woman feels unable to get her point across or articulate her views, every time she is silenced by being ignored or interrupted in a meeting or corporate or political event, she is not heard and her ideas are lost. Worst case scenario: this starts to undermine the perception of her credibility and creates a self-fulfilling prophesy around her competence.

For millennial women who are early in their career, or perhaps just getting their first senior roles, feeling less willing and able to speak up or speak out and feeling like it is a struggle to be heard can have a massive impact on their careers and, therefore, on gender equality too.

Not speaking up makes it much harder for women to influence, persuade and succeed. It makes them less organisationally visible and lessens their opportunity to build credibility and reputation. This in turn makes it harder for women to achieve their aims and reach the more senior roles, which perpetuates inequality and gender imbalance.

Why does speaking matter to gender equality?

Speaking is key to professional success and if women do not feel comfortable doing it, that negatively affects not only their individual careers, but also the wider advancement of women.

Equality is important to a thriving and successful modern society. Gender inequality is unfair and unproductive. How can you maximise the UK's, or any other country's, national productivity when half of the population is underengaged and underutilised?

Acknowledgement of this is, in itself, incontrovertible.

So, what's all the fuss about? The battle for gender equality is already won isn't it? The equal rights, equal pay, anti-discrimination legislation is all in place. True. To assume there is no problem, however, is an easy trap for millennial women to fall into.

I started work in the late 80s with leading female figures abundantly on display: the Queen, the Prime Minister and Madonna, to name a few. I remember the story at the time of a small child asking her mother: 'Mummy, are men allowed to be prime ministers?' I did not think too much about equality issues at the time. I subconsciously assumed that had been taken care of by the feminists in the 60s and 70s – job done. Carrie Gracie (the BBC journalist whose book *Equal* [5] details her struggle to get equal pay from the BBC) also talks about this: 'When I joined the workforce in the 1980s, powerful women seemed to bestride the world. I simply assumed that every woman of my generation would be treated as equal.' If women entering the workplace in the 1980s felt they would be treated equally, of course it's not surprising that millennial women, born in the first two decades of the 21st century, would assume the world has moved on since then and therefore have even greater expectations of gender equality.

However, the problem is not solved. The issues have just become more subtle, less obvious. The barriers to equality are now like the rocks below the surface of the water rather than the hazards that can be clearly seen. Dealing with overt discrimination, as the women of the 60s and 70s had to, was in some respects easier because the issues were clearer. It was demonstrably unfair to pay women less when they were in exactly the same job as men. Nowadays, the gender pay gap is still wide: in 2019 the gap was 17.3% in the UK (ie for every £1 men were paid, women were paid £0.83) but the reasons for this are subtle and not quite so clear cut as before.[6] The nuances of job evaluations and job comparisons, for example, are often where the issues lie today.

The danger is that the millennial generation is fighting the same battles as the previous one. They are getting tangled in the same issues because they think the issues are no longer there, when in reality, they absolutely are. All that has really changed is that the manifestations of the old issues are just more subtle and harder to identify.

The challenge for millennial women is to recognise these issues early on, and be willing and able to speak up, challenge and/or navigate them consciously rather than wait until they 'run aground on the rocks' later in their careers.

We are still so far from equality. More than 100 years on from women in the UK gaining the vote, in 2020 the proportion of women is still only 34% in the UK parliament and 35% in local government.[7] In the US, only 23% of the House of Representatives and 22% of the Senate are female.[8] In the UK, women's representation in local government is 'at a standstill', according to the Fawcett Society[9], and 29.5% of FTSE 250 board members are women.[10] In the US, women still only make up 20% of boards. Globally, women still carry the majority (75%) of all unpaid/caring work in the world.[11]

In her book *Invisible Women*, Caroline Criado-Perez lays out an incredibly detailed, data-backed exposition of how the world is designed by and for men, because that is the way it's always been. She points out that many data sets are not disaggregated so you cannot even see the difference between men and women. It is a massive data gap which creates unconscious bias and discrimination. Ever stood in the queue for a public toilet? I would think every woman, bar the Queen, has and does regularly. This is something that I've just taken as a fact of life and never even thought to question why it should be. Perhaps it is because engineers and building designers are, and certainly have historically been, predominantly male. These male designers have not had (or looked at) the data on women and toilet usage, hence there are never enough.

Without the data or the perspective of female engineers on their team, how could they be expected to know? If they had seen the data on how much longer women need in toilets compared to men, then maybe there would be adequate provision. This is classic unconscious bias. Caroline Criado-Perez outlines how everything from buildings with insufficient women's toilets to car safety, taxation frameworks, drug development and military and police equipment are all designed around the concept of men as the default human beings and women as the anomalies.[12]

Speaking in public is critical to women's personal and group progress and the factors that effectively silence women and cause their voices not to be heard are similar to Criado-Perez's invisible data gap.

The reasons are there. They are real (although not highly visible). They affect women daily. They create unconscious bias, which means women have a hard time being heard.

When women don't speak in meetings or in presentations, they:

- don't get credit for their work and ideas (somebody else does)

- don't get visibility

- don't get considered for promotion

- don't get seen as leadership material

This then gets in the way of women's progress and gender equality and goes some way towards explaining the slow pace of progress towards full equality.

Fix the system, not the women

> The reasonable man adapts himself to the world, the unreasonable one persists in trying to adapt the world to himself. Therefore, all progress depends on the unreasonable man.
>
> **George Bernard Shaw, *Man and Superman***

This book is designed to be a handbook for individual women. Many might argue that we should not focus on individual women and what they can or should be doing. Surely, we should fix the system, not the women?

Criado-Perez makes the point that because the male is often the 'default human' and women the 'exception', the onus is usually on women to adapt, be trained or change themselves. For example, the female police officer being told to stop 'whining' and just get used to the ill-fitting stab vests that fail to keep her safe. This is clearly absurd. It is in fact the system, the data, the algorithm or the design that need to change, not the women. I fully agree with her point.

Creating the change is a challenge. That change could be advocating for more women to be involved in clinical trials to know how drugs affect women versus men. It could be design teams taking account of women's different shape in order to create protective equipment that fits. It could be governments adapting fiscal policy to recognise women's time out of the workforce for childbirth. But here's the thing about speaking: *effecting any of these things requires women to speak up and advocate for change.*

On a more personal level, getting the recognition and promotions women earn and deserve, and making personal progress and maximising their own potential also requires women to speak up and speak out. If they do not, or if they do and are not heard, the system, paradigms, datasets and algorithms will not change.

In the ongoing struggle for gender equality there is a huge case for systemic change. There is also a parallel need for individual women to be willing and able to speak up effectively and advocate for change, and to influence and persuade men to join them to create that fairer and more productive future that benefits all of society, both men and women.

This book is not about placing blame on women for not speaking out or for saying they are in any way flawed and must 'fix' themselves. There is no suggestion that women, collectively or individually, are broken or inadequate in how they communicate. Neither is this a Henry Higgins moment of saying 'Why can't a woman be more like a man?'[13] and that women should change themselves to replicate the way men communicate.

I see the issues as circular. Women's willingness and ability to speak up and be heard is critical to:

a. their personal success and fulfilment

b. gender equality

Individual women may be interested in their personal success or the wider issue of gender equality, or both, but in any case, it starts with the ability to speak and be heard.

Where women are interested in gender equality, it's fair to say that achieving equality does need societal change (campaigning and role modelling, gathering support and creating a critical mass) but it starts with individual women taking ownership.

Stephen Covey, in his excellent book *7 Habits of Highly Successful People*, talks about everyone having three concentric circles in their lives. The biggest is the circle of concern, in which you place things that are of concern to you but that you cannot directly control, like climate change, or pandemic diseases. The next is the circle of influence, ie things that you cannot control but on which you can have some influence, like pay policy at your company or a planning permission in your local area. Finally, there is the circle of control, which contains the things you directly control, such as your job, your exercise, what you spend etc.

His message is essentially: don't dissipate time worrying about areas you can't do anything about. If you focus on what you can control and get really excellent at that, then you will grow the size of your area of influence and ultimately even be able to impact wider areas of concern.

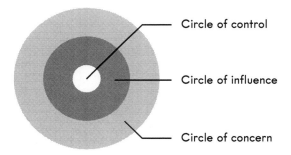

In the context of speaking in public, you can't change all of the societal norms that have been ingrained over thousands of years, but you can control how and when you speak up and if you do that effectively, even powerfully, you will grow your influence and your ability to challenge and change those norms.

So, this book is not about 'fixing' women, it is about making yourself best able to be effective and successful and build your career. It also means that if you want to, you will also be better placed to advocate for change.

.

CHAPTER 2

The 4,000-year silence project

_____

So, where are you? Do you dislike having to speak up in public or large meetings, giving presentations or speeches? Do you try to avoid it where possible? Or perhaps you don't mind speaking, but when you do speak up, it can feel like wading through treacle. It can feel like it's a fight to be fully 'heard'. Somehow, it feels like you are not taken quite as seriously as the men in the room. Or maybe you don't have any of these feelings?

Many millennial women I've spoken with in their 20s or early 30s and the early years of their career would often say at first: 'No, it's fine, I don't have any issues with speaking in public.' But as they progress, they increasingly start to mirror the experiences of many older women, which is that it all seems OK at first, then as you get more established and more senior you become more and more aware of some of the challenges involved in being fully heard.

It starts to feel harder and more of an uphill struggle as you seek to navigate and overcome the subtle barriers and issues that get in the way of your speaking out and being heard and therefore as effective and successful as you would like. It feels like navigating the ship of your career through rock- and iceberg-strewn waters where many of the hazards are out of sight, just below the water.

Sheryl Sandberg, Carrie Gracie and many other women have spoken about coming late to this awareness of the gender-related barriers they faced.

Where you are in your career may alter your perception of the challenges, so let's explore those challenges.

Why do so many women feel like they just do not like speaking? Why do they feel it is so hard to be heard?

The first thing to understand is the historical context. There is a 4,000-year-old conspiracy to keep women quiet. That may sound a bit dramatic, but, in essence, it is true.

4,000 years of silence

We don't need a doctorate in anthropology to know that historically men have been the dominant sex. They have held the power, the money and the leadership positions.

In ancient civilisations, where all was dependent on physical strength and ability to dominate others, society was of course going to be led and built around men as the physically stronger sex. In the days of blood feuds and tribal warfare, strength counted. It often seems that much of history is, in fact, the history of war and conflict and up until very recently that meant being able to fight and be physically strong. So, fair enough, these are sound, understandable, historical reasons for the patriarchy that has been in place since time immemorial and the justifiably essential framework for how the world has worked for millennia.

The world, however, has changed. The prevalence of physical strength as a major societal factor is no longer relevant. At the very least, physical strength is massively less significant in developed societies. You can fight a war in Afghanistan with drones controlled by a light joystick from a pod on an airbase in Arizona. The 21st century knowledge economy requires brains, not brawn.

So, is it even worth looking back at the historical context, then? Yes, it is, because our history has shaped and continues to highly influence our social norms and paradigms. Cultural norms can and do take generations to change.

To this day, those paradigms subconsciously shape our thoughts, our beliefs and our actions. I often equate this to our hardwiring. You don't see the circuitry but it's there beneath the surface and it drives the operation of the machine (us!). In Chapter 1, I mentioned that when I ask women why they don't like speaking up in meetings and events they often say they don't know why, they just don't like it. Understanding the historical context can help us understand why many women feel this way.

A brief scan of the history

In one of the oldest sets of laws ever recorded − on the Enmetena and Urukagina cones (*c.*2400 BC) − one of the laws addressed a speech code for women which specified that a woman speaking out of turn to a man should 'have her teeth smashed by a burnt brick'! This is shocking, but true. In Ancient Greece, Homer labelled speech 'the business of men'. Sophocles wrote 'silence is a woman's garment'.

The classicist Mary Beard, in the book *Women & Power: A Manifesto* 2017, describes the situation in the ancient world where speaking was in fact not just something predominantly only men did, but more than that. It was actually 'a defining attribute of maleness'. Only men could and did speak in public. A woman speaking was therefore an aberration, an unnatural phenomenon, a freak show!

Given how much of western cultural tradition is founded on the thinking of the ancient Greeks, understanding this is important. Mary Beard captured it by saying that this exclusion of women from public speaking is something that has 'a much greater impact than we usually acknowledge on our traditions, conventions and assumptions about the voice of women'.[14]

The Christian Bible went on to perpetuate this belief in women's silence. The Creation story that has Eve as the root of all evil for tempting Adam away from the perfect and idyllic garden of Eden set the stage for an Old Testament that was heavy on the misogyny of the time. Women were seen as an evil necessity who should be silenced and kept very much in their place – witness the following quotes:

- 'From a garment comes a moth, from women wickedness.' (Ecclesiastes 42:13)

- In the New Testament, St Paul writes to the Corinthians that 'women should remain silent in churches. They are not allowed to speak but must be in submission…' (1 Corinthians 14:34) '… for it is disgraceful for a woman to speak in church.' (1 Corinthians 14:35)

- Paul also writes to Timothy: 'A woman must learn in quietness and full submissiveness' (1 Timothy 2:11) and 'I do not permit a woman to teach or exercise authority over a man; she is to remain quiet.' (1 Timothy 2:12).

To this very day in the UK, some men will leave a church rather than listen to a female vicar. I heard recently of a conflict that arose between a female vicar and a family over their father's dying wish not to be buried by a female vicar. Despite the fact that in the Church of England congregations are predominantly (about 65%) female, 70% of vicars are men, the ordination of women is only 26 years old, the consecration of female bishops only six years old and no woman has yet been made an archbishop.

John Knox, the 16th-century founder of the Presbyterian Church of Scotland, was a later proponent of this same school of thought. His famous tract *The First Blast of the Trumpet Against the Monstrous Regiment of Women* rails against female monarchs, arguing that rule by females is contrary to the Bible. In it, he says that 'God, by the order of his creation, has [deprived] woman of authority and dominion' and 'man has seen, proved, and pronounced just causes why it should be.'

The 19th-century suffragette movement campaigning to secure votes for women met with routine criticism for being outspoken, noisy and therefore 'unladylike'. Despite a parliamentary system where the House of Commons regularly featured male political opponents shouting at each other across the green benches, it was unacceptable for women to protest assertively.

Even in the early days of the women's suffrage campaigns when suffragettes merely heckled government ministers in 1906, they were often treated with violence and manhandled roughly by the police. In December 1908, when suffragettes broke up a Women's Liberal Federation meeting at the Royal Albert Hall in London where Lloyd-George, the then Chancellor of the Exchequer, was speaking, the newspaper *The Observer* commented that the 'shrieking women' had turned the event into 'a Bedlam... all sense of decency lost... it was a melancholy and disheartening spectacle.'[15] It was clear that women did not have society's permission to speak out for what they believed in.

Millicent Fawcett's suffragist movement was the forerunner of the suffragettes; they were more moderate and 'ladylike'. They were, however, thoroughly ignored and not listened to by the male political establishment for decades. It could be argued that the ignoring of women's voices was what led to the formation and rise of Mrs Pankhurst's more radical suffragette movement and their resorting to increasingly violent tactics. It is perhaps no coincidence that the quieter Fawcett is the one whose statue has been erected outside the Houses of Parliament in Westminster

Square (the first female statue there). We are clearly still not comfortable with outspoken women today.

We can clearly see that the silencing of women has been a 4,000-year-old project, a clear and consistent pattern whose progress can be traced from ancient times to more recent history.

The situation today

But surely this is no longer the case in the modern era? Surely, despite this historical backdrop, silence is no longer an expectation of women in developed society?

Women have been leaders, UK prime ministers (twice), First Minister of Scotland, ministers, bishops and CEOs. Women's rights campaigns have been successful in establishing a legislative environment that makes it illegal to discriminate against women.

However, the subtle underlying cultural pressures to silence women remain.

Hillary Clinton, in her book *What Happened* wrote: 'Sexism is all the big and little ways that society draws a box around women and says, "you stay there, don't complain because nice girls don't do that. Don't try and be something women shouldn't be."'[16] You may call this pressure for women to be silent unconscious bias or outright sexism. The truth, as always, lies somewhere in between.

The proof of this is simply that men speak much more than women; in fact men speak 75% of the time in decision-making groups.[17] It is still men who make up the majority of speakers we hear in almost all aspects of life.

At conferences:

- 69% of speakers in conferences worldwide are male (in the UK it is worse, 75% are male)

  o This research analysed the gender diversity of more than 60,000 event speakers over a five-year period, from 2013 to 2018. The study spanned 23 countries and thousands of the world's largest professional events.

  o The research includes people speaking at all forms of public speaking events in business, trade shows, networking events, internal events, fundraising or gala events. Only in fundraising events were half (54%) of the speakers women.[18]

In the media:

- The majority of TV news presenters are men. Figures from analysis done by MP Harriet Harman in 2013 showed that women only made up 39% of all presenters. Those numbers dropped dramatically after the age of 50 with women representing only 18% of all presenters.[19]

- Of all the TV coverage (ordinary people, expert pollsters, businesspeople and union people), 76%

consisted of men speaking. Men spoke three times more than women on the TV and five times more in newspaper coverage.

In politics:

- Only 20% of the speakers and commentators/participants at Davos are women.

- Globally, there are only 24% of women in national parliaments. In the UK it is 33%.

- Of the 20 most prominent spokespeople in the media coverage in the first week of the 2019 UK general election, only five were women.

The Australian organisation Panel Pledge summarises this lack of female visibility in speakers as a vicious circle and a self-fulfilling prophesy by saying: 'Since speakers are usually male, audiences are given a narrow perspective. Fewer women choose to speak, and fewer are chosen. Without the opportunity for women to serve on panels as thought leaders, women lack profile-building speaking opportunities, an important contributor to experience and recognition.'

When women actually do speak up, in meetings and in Q&A sessions, they are much more likely to get shouted down and interrupted. Whether this is done consciously or subconsciously, the net effect is the same: it is a very effective method of silencing them.

Research proves that on average women get interrupted twice as often as men. Interestingly, women are interrupted by both men and other women, suggesting that the societal norm which says women should not really speak up is subconsciously accepted by both sexes.

For instance, one study analysed 31 separate two-part conversations, 10 of which were between two men, 10 others between two women, and the remaining 11 between a man and a woman. The researchers identified seven interruptions overall in the two same-sex groups combined; in the male-female groups, however, the researchers found 48 total interruptions – and 46 of them were instigated by the man. [20]

According to 2019 annual research conducted by McKinsey for the Lean In organisation, men experience being interrupted when they speak 34% of the time. Women get interrupted 50% of the time, ie every other time they speak![21]

This has certainly been my experience in the business world, and that of virtually all the women I interviewed. Interestingly, it is such ingrained behaviour that when people do this to me, it's often perfectly pleasant, civilised people who simply do not realise they are even doing it and they are often mortified if I point it out. Others who interrupt and begin 'mansplaining' (ie explaining in a patronising way something that the woman concerned already knows) are doing it more as a conscious power or status display. This can make women feel their contribution has been dismissed or not valued, which in turn does not encourage further participation. All of this amounts to subtle but powerful silencing.

The trouble with this is that once women have been interrupted, they then tend to stay out of the ensuing discussion, fearing that to reassert themselves back into the conversation risks attracting criticism and being perceived as defensive, 'shrill' or 'strident' women.

Why are women silenced?

Men interrupt more partly because they feel they are entitled to it, partly because they can and are used to getting away with it, and partly because of the style differences in communication. Men in professional settings tend to compete while women collaborate. When women communicate, they focus more on listening, collaboration and two-way communication; their interactions tend to be less combative and adversarial than men's.

However, the whole nature of western democracy is founded on the ancient Greek concept of rhetorical conflict: thesis, antithesis and synthesis. This is the concept that you have an idea (thesis), somebody puts forward the opposite case to that idea (antithesis) and out of the argument eventually comes some useful compromise or output (synthesis). The UK Parliament institutionalises that and physically embodies it with the benches that face each other from opposing sides, the concept of Her Majesty's opposition, and the shouting and heckling. None of that is the way women would typically choose to go about things. They have, however, adapted to it.

In the 1997 election the number of women MPs leapt from 60 to 120. This was due to the introduction of all-women shortlists in the Labour Party and the advent of the subsequent cohort of female MPs dubbed by the media, in classically sexist fashion, 'Blair's babes'.

There was some research done in Westminster in 1999 which looked at the behaviours of female MPs and how they fared in the bear pit environment of parliamentary debate. It concluded that women asked the same number of questions and did adjust to the adversarial culture, but that they did not interrupt as much as men. (They are 'good girls' and play by the rules: technically, interrupting is against parliamentary rules, yet most male MPs do it all the time and it is a powerful way to be heard.) Men interrupted 10 times more than women. The net effect was men's overall contribution to debates ended up being 66% of the total.[22]

Another factor that silences women in the modern world is the fact that those women who do speak up are often subjected to vitriolic, personal criticism that is designed to shut them up. You need look no further than Donald Trump to see this spectacularly in action. In January 2020, 50 congresswomen wrote to him to protest against how he seeks to 'humiliate and silence any woman who fights back, speaks up or takes up space'.[23] Trump is admittedly an extreme case, bordering on a caricature, but there are endless instances of determined and assertive women being dismissed: Prime Minister Theresa May was derided by one of her own cabinet colleagues, Ken Clarke, as 'a bloody difficult woman'. I will explore this further in the chapter on criticism (Chapter 5).

In her fight for equal pay at the BBC, Carrie Gracie was about to appear at a parliamentary select committee when she was advised by a friend, a senior civil servant, 'not to threaten the men'. This sends some clear messages to women: speaking is risky, if you must speak up then you have to be extremely careful because you'll probably offend people who essentially think you should be quiet.

Even when women do speak, they are sometimes unwittingly complicit in perpetuating the assumption that women should not really speak up. Women adapt to the system, to the machine, they bend themselves out of shape and engage in the exhausting process of constant self-editing. Sheryl Sandberg captured this in *Lean In: Women, Work and the Will to Lead*, saying: 'Women... believe that men at the top are entitled to be there so they try and play by the rules and work harder rather than trying to raise questions or voice concerns.' [24]

All of this clearly demonstrates that at a mostly unconscious, societal level both men and, significantly, women themselves do not believe women have an equal right to speak. This is the ingrained cultural backdrop that works against women speaking up and speaking out.

It is therefore easy for women to see speaking out and speaking up as a not particularly 'natural', perhaps slightly unfeminine, thing for women to do. In the old saying, 'it's hard to be what you don't see.' For many women, the decision not to speak up is not a conscious thought but merely an automated, logical conclusion reached on the basis of societal norms and what they observe and internalise on a day-to-day basis in the world around them.

In summary, the 4,000-year silence project, the cultural paradigms millennial women live with can:

- cause women to feel a subtle, unspoken pressure not to speak

- cause women to feel unduly anxious when they do speak

- cause others (men and women) to feel that women should not really be speaking up and therefore feel free to interrupt them, not listen to them or disproportionately challenge them

- make women feel it is a struggle to be taken seriously and fully 'heard'

What to do

In the world of coaching there is a phrase that 'awareness is curative'. This means that once you become fully aware of a situation or a context you will naturally adjust and adapt to improve it.

Tactics to navigate

Be aware

Whatever environment you work in, whether business, politics, public sector, schools or voluntary organisations, start by keeping a record somewhere over a period of a few weeks of how many men as opposed to women you see speaking in meetings/presentations, etc. This will build your awareness that just because you see more men speaking, it doesn't mean you should not.

Amplify

Draw attention to interruptions and amplify other women.

In *Lean In: Women, Work and the Will to* Lead, Sheryl Sandberg talks about Ken Chenault, former CEO of American Express, who acknowledges that men and women are more likely to interrupt women and often give credit to a man for an idea first proposed by a woman (the Miss Triggs phenomenon). Sandberg says that to combat this, as a leader, Chenault makes a point of calling it out whenever he sees it happen, by stopping a meeting to point it out and allow the interrupted woman to finish her point. If you're running or chairing a meeting, you should be alert to this and prepared to challenge it.

In fact, this can also be done as a participant. You can politely and calmly draw attention to the interruption (without attacking the interrupter) when you notice this happening to a woman. For example: 'I don't think Mary quite had the chance to finish making her point but it sounded like the beginning of a good idea. Mary, would you finish your point?' This will start raising people's (both men's and women's) awareness of the importance of not interrupting, and will both encourage women and create a more positive environment for all.

Airspace

A related point is paying attention to the 'airspace' factor: how often are men speaking in meetings as opposed to women? An entertaining way to do this is by using the tool you can find on www.arementalkingtoomuch.com. It allows you to push a button that records when someone is speaking and at the end gives you a percentage split of how much men spoke versus women. You then have to adjust for the proportion of men and women in the meeting, and the results are interesting.

You can use this just for your own awareness and as encouragement to speak more, or you can share it with colleagues to start raising awareness of the airspace issue, which might encourage men to let more women speak, perhaps even invite them to!

Actively seek out speaking opportunities

Always accept speaking invitations for presentations and speeches and grasp opportunities to speak up in meetings. Volunteer to speak at conferences. This may push you out of your comfort zone but recognise that being in that comfort zone is a place of restriction that will do you no favours. Speak up, speak out, be heard:

- tell your story, or someone else will – you are the best person to talk about your work

- build up your skills to feel more confident – the more you do it, the better you will get at speaking

You will worry less and your skills and confidence will grow. It is important to tackle this at the beginning of your career, as it is a way to accelerate your progress towards career success and the achievement of your goals.

Tactics to challenge

Handle interruptions

Notice if you ever feel silenced by interruptions. Notice it for what it is – an interruption – and try to just continue making your point. If you are not allowed to, calmly challenge the interruption. Find some words and phrases you're comfortable with to push back on the interruption. This needs to be in your style and in a way that you feel is mostly likely to succeed in your work context. Some examples could be:

- 'I'd appreciate the chance to finish my point.'

- 'Wait a second, please let me finish.'

- 'Give me one more minute to finish my point, then I'm interested to hear your point of view.'

- 'Hold on, I haven't got to the good bit yet!'

- 'I'm glad you're so eager to contribute, but please do let me finish my thought.'

- 'I'm sure you didn't mean to interrupt me so if I could finish my point, which was...'

The important thing is not to let go and fail to make your point or share your idea. It is tempting to think it's not worth struggling against the interrupters, that you'll find another way to make your point at a later time. This becomes an ingrained habit and is a major reason why people continue to interrupt, which is an effective way to dominate the conversation. Perhaps you should take a moment to consider, maybe even jot down, your preferred phrase or phrases to address this.

Come back to your point

If you are interrupted, you could choose not to challenge the person interrupting you right away, but always make sure you come back to it. It's worth jotting down a quick note so you don't forget your point, and it reminds you to raise it again when there is an opportunity.

Develop thick skin

Recognise that to get the things you want and need to achieve done you may have to be prepared to be 'a difficult woman'.

Challenge all-male panels/speaker line-ups

Call out 'manspanels'. Challenge the lack of gender balance where you see it on lists of speakers or panels. Where you see it, contact organisers and ask them why there were no female panellists.

Interrupt

In meeting environments, interrupting may not be strictly playing by the rules but it is often a powerful way to be heard. Being a compliant good girl who raises her hand in the style of Harry Potter's Hermione Granger may work at school but is not effective at work in mixed groups. If it does not come naturally (as it does not to many women), develop some language that enables you to interrupt when you need to assert yourself at the meeting. Making use of smooth segues, such as the ones below, is a good skill:

- 'I agree broadly with your point, but a much bigger point / issue/ concern is… '

- 'To build on that, I'd say…'

- 'But on that point…'

CHAPTER 3

The princess and the imposter

_____

'Once upon a time in a land much like yours and mine, lived a young girl named Ella. She was born in a small house where she lived with her mother, Lily, and her father, a hardworking merchant. Her mother was kind, loving and patient, and her father was successful. His success allowed them to move into a large, four thousand-acre estate…'

As we all know, it all went horribly wrong for Cinderella, but later in the same story…

"Who is that?" called the familiar voice. Cinderella turned around and caught a glimpse of the handsome blue eyes looking up at her. The man from the ball _was_ the prince.

"Ella," she replied softly. "Ella," the prince repeated. He walked carefully into the manor and greeted her with an outstretched hand. He gently slipped the glass slipper on her foot: the perfect match. Without a word, he led her away from her stunned wicked stepfamily and into the royal carriage. "You are enchanting," he said, looking into Ella's eyes… and they lived happily ever after…'

Cinderella, Sleeping Beauty, Snow White, Belle from *Beauty and the Beast*, the Little Mermaid – Disney princesses are the stuff of childhood for many girls as they grow up. They capture a paradigm of what society thinks little girls might want to grow up to be: beautiful, demure damsels who, regardless of their distress, nonetheless manage to look elegant in gorgeous frocks, capturing the heart of a handsome prince who will save them from whatever foe they face (from dragons to wicked stepmothers). He will then whisk them off and look after them for the rest of their lives, happily ever after.

This captures the stylised cultural paradigms of society's expectations of women: pleasant, compliant and basically there for decoration! You can see this historically in hundreds of song lyrics, but one that stands out is Gershwin's *Summertime*: 'Summertime, and the livin' is easy, fish are jumpin', and the cotton is high, oh your daddy's rich and your ma is good lookin', so hush, little baby, don't you cry.' So that's clear then, as long as your mum looks good, all is well!

But that's all changed now, hasn't it? We have all kinds of equality legislation, female prime ministers, we have Oprah and Beyoncé, for heaven's sake! Those old-fashioned paradigms, where a woman's worth was judged and valued predominantly based on her looks, don't affect millennial women anymore, do they?[25]

Firstly, do not underestimate the power of these social stereotypes that are ingrained in young women from the cradle onwards. They are ingrained in childhood, where we just absorb the messaging into our belief system before the power of critical thought kicks in. Secondly, although we live in the age of equality legislation, these paradigms have become worse, not better. Smartphones that take photos and social media to distribute them have only heightened society's obsession with appearance.

The princess paradigm is all tied up with appearance. The good characters are the beautiful princesses and the baddies are the ugly sisters. It encourages the tendency to judge women predominantly by appearance.

I could not help thinking of this recently when the Duchess of Cambridge published some adorable pictures of her children for their birthdays. Prince George was pictured in his England football shirt, looking like he'd just had a good rough and tumble on the pitch. Prince Louis had his hands messily and delightfully covered in paint as he created finger-painted rainbows. Princess Charlotte was prim and pretty. Immaculately dressed in a pretty dress, not a hair out of place. The princess paradigm is alive and well in 2020!

The pressure on the Instagram generation of young women to constantly post picture-perfect images of themselves has become a huge phenomenon. For young people, and particularly young girls, being liked and approved of on social media is what life is all about, and the way you get that approval is to post those perfect selfies.

The pervasiveness and easy availability of online porn is also a dynamic that encourages generations of younger men to see women mainly in terms of their appearance and sexual value. Some would argue it has increased the objectification of women.

Despite all the advances of women's equality, there are many phenomena pulling women and equality backwards as there are drivers pushing it forwards. There is still a deeply ingrained paradigm in society that expects women and girls to be 'sugar and spice and all things nice'.

The perfection trap

What impact does the princess paradigm have on women's willingness and ability to speak up and speak out?

It is this cultural paradigm that encourages girls and women to feel like they need to be perfect, to be immaculate and to be people pleasers. To do that requires putting others first, never offending, always looking immaculate and excelling at all the expected female caring roles (housekeeping, caring for your children and/or elderly parents) as well as all your academic or career roles.

Women internalise the message that they need to be good girls, and if they are, then the affirmation and rewards come their way. This requirement of perfection is utterly exhausting and the phenomenon of burnout and ill health in women is a growing problem.

In the context of speaking in public, this means:

- women are often less inclined to take risks and speaking up in public is risky

- women do not want to speak up unless what they have to say is 'perfect'

- women constantly feel inadequate and that they are 'not very good at speaking'

Let's look at each of these points.

Speaking up and taking risks

Speaking up does contain an element of risk. Public speaking often comes in at number 1 or 2 in terms of people's biggest fears. Seventy-four per cent of people (men and women) have glossophobia (it's a thing, honestly, it means the fear of public speaking). In fact, it's sometimes been said that people hate speaking so much that if asked to give a funeral eulogy, they'd rather be in the coffin than give the speech! Steven Spielberg once said that after he'd done all the scary scenes of *Raiders of the Lost Ark* with various creepy crawlies, terrifying monsters and horrifying ancient tombs, to go even more scary the next time he was going to do a film about public speaking!

When you speak, whether it is in a meeting, presentation or speech, all eyes are on you. All attention is on you. The pressure is on you. You are exposed.

This can provoke anxiety in everyone, but it is more intimidating for women because of the cultural norms. Reshma Saujani, founder of Girls who Code, wrote a book called *Brave, not Perfect*. In it, she argues that we raise girls to be perfect and boys to be brave. If little girls are the confection and perfection of sugar and spice, it means that the world acknowledges and praises perfect little girls while boys get to be all about 'frogs and snails and puppy dogs' tails'; they get to charge around getting into scrapes and getting things wrong, but that's OK because they have the universal get of jail free card: 'boys will be boys'. [26]

This pressure on women and girls to be perfect causes them to be cautious. There is huge subconscious pressure to not mess up, and therefore speaking up is a potentially huge risk. If the topic is uncontroversial and the audience small and familiar to you, then maybe that pressure isn't too great. If, however, you are speaking up to challenge or disagree with something, expressing something controversial or a minority point of view, speaking to a large group or audience or to people not known to you, then it can be scary and represent a risk. What if everyone disagrees with you? What if you make a mistake, get your facts wrong or stumble when articulating the point? What impact will that have on your credibility, your reputation, your career?

When you see it like this, it is little wonder public speaking in all its forms can be scary for both men and women. It can require courage to put yourself out there and speak up, yet many women have been subconsciously socialised to be cautious and not risk takers.

This caution, this risk aversion is the reason why many women decline opportunities to speak. I have known countless women who are brilliant at their job, very successful, have boundless knowledge and wisdom to share who, when invited to speak at a company kick-off meeting or industry event, will do almost anything rather than get up on a stage and talk about it. They find a reason to be abroad that day, or suddenly have a diary full of 'must-do' meetings or they pass the speaking gig on to a junior colleague, saying 'It'll be good development for them!'

The issue, however, is that those speaking opportunities are critical to career and reputation building. It is often the time when the wider organisation gets to see you. It is the time when you get to showcase your achievements and ideas and earn recognition for them. Turning down those opportunities is a tragedy and absolutely does not help women in career advancement and breaking that glass ceiling.

That is why this book is designed to help women develop the willingness and ability to seize those opportunities to speak up and speak out.

Keeping quiet unless you have something 'perfect' to say

There's plenty of research that proves that many women will not apply for a job unless they feel they meet 100% of the job specification criteria, whereas men will have a go if they meet 60% of the criteria.

Similarly, women will often not seek to speak up in a meeting until and unless they are 100% sure of their point and have the argument well developed. They want their answer to be well researched, accurate and data-backed. In meetings and question and answer (Q&A) situations, the chances of having something 'perfect' to say in the moment is rare. By the time the idea or response is fully thought out, perhaps jotted down in neat bullet points, the opportunity to speak may have passed, resulting in fewer women being heard and fewer points of views considered, which can lead to less effective solutions. One woman I interviewed, a marketing director, says she felt she had to have 'something amazing to say' before making an intervention in a noisy meeting.

Women are less likely to volunteer an opinion than men. Various studies have shown that in environments where a question is thrown out to a group (for example in MBA lectures, training courses or meetings, or when a consultant is doing the rounds with medical students) the men are more likely than the women to be the first to offer an answer. They tend to be more confident, assertive and competitive in pushing themselves forward to answer.

Is this a matter of women's confidence? Do women on average simply have less confidence than men? And more specifically, is that true of millennial women? I believe the answer is: absolutely not!

It is not lack of confidence in their own abilities that makes women less proactive in answering questions and contributing to discussions. In fact, there have been many studies that show that when women are specifically asked, they give answers that are at least as confident and competent as those of the men.

What is true it that men and women's confidence manifests itself differently. The flipside of the princess paradigm is the prince principle: men grow up learning that they must be strong, powerful and assertive. Even if they don't necessarily feel this way, they are taught that they must mask it, 'man-up' and appear to be brave and strong. They also are socialised to believe that if they make a mistake, it is not the end of the world; they can laugh it off and move on.

This leads to many men displaying confidence in a loud, brash fashion. A man who is outspoken, makes bold statements and is totally sure of himself is seen as charismatic and leadership material.

Over the course of history, we have seen the bold, the extrovert and the visibly confident men as leaders. That is the way it has always been, so we have come to equate confidence with competence. To be successful, men are socialised to be big, bold and confident regardless of how they feel. They are used to having to fake it.

Women, on the other hand, have been socialised to be more demure, not to be loud and brash (that would not be at all princess-like!), so even when women, and particularly millennial women, are highly confident of their own abilities and competence, they don't normally display it in quite the same way. Their confidence is more of an internal self-belief than an overt, outward-facing display of self-confidence.

The problem is that because society has conflated competence with confidence, when women don't speak up and speak out they are seen as less competent, less of a good leader and as having less potential.

Professor of business psychology Tomas Chamorro-Premuzic talks about this confidence effect and reflects on research which shows that 'we are, it seems, less likely to tolerate high confidence in women. This bias creates a lose-lose situation for women.' Outspoken, confident speaking in women is likely to be judged negatively as pushy or arrogant.

This explains why women often choose not to speak up or actively volunteer their views and ideas.

Women's imposter syndrome

The other big effect of the pressure to be perfect is a constant feeling of inadequacy. If only 100% is acceptable to you, that's a tough place to be, as life rarely permits things to be perfect all or even most of the time. That feeling of shame, of never being good enough, of being a fraud and never quite worthy of whatever it is you have achieved has a name: it is known as 'imposter syndrome'.

I once ran an event in the House of Commons for women who were potential MP candidates. The audience consisted of some 40 women who had achieved senior roles in business and politics and had passed rigorous assessments to get themselves in a position to be selected for political office. I asked these impressive ladies: 'Who's heard of imposter syndrome?' and most hands went up. I then asked: 'Who has suffered at any stage from the feelings of inferiority that are symptomatic of the imposter syndrome?' and almost all hands went up again. At first glance, it was extraordinary that these accomplished women had all felt inadequate at least some of the time.

They are not alone, however. Many brilliant women such as Maya Angelou, Emma Watson and Oprah Winfrey have also been open about discussing their battles with imposter syndrome. Another woman who questioned her significant abilities is Emma Walmsley, the CEO of pharmaceutical giant GSK. She is the first female chief executive of the £80-billion company and arguably the most powerful woman in British business. When she got the role in 2016 she said: 'I spent a week persuading myself I would be insane to do it,' adding that she asked herself: 'Am I really qualified? How could a mum and a wife take on something so big?' She accepted after her husband 'gently reminded me that every time I'd taken a new role, I had constantly told him it was too big for me and then managed fine'.

Imposter syndrome is a remarkably common and pervasive psychological pattern in which an individual doubts his or her accomplishments and has a persistent internalised fear of being exposed as a 'fraud'. Apparently, 70% of people have experienced this at some stage of their lives.[27] You know you are suffering from imposter syndrome when you live with the fear that the 'competency police' will bust in at any moment and take you away!

Many women fear that if they stick their head above the parapet by standing up to speak they will be exposed. Their thought process goes: 'People will see me, I'll be exposed, they'll clearly see what I've always known, that I'm not quite good enough. I'm not actually the perfect person I've been pretending to be. They'll know I've just been lucky; I don't really deserve to be here, and I am not actually worth listening to.' Both men and women suffer from imposter syndrome, but women typically suffer more because of this 'perfect princess' factor.

Many millennial women suffer badly from this. There has been research which suggests that 70% of young people suffer from this and that it is getting worse, not better. That has been caused by a number of factors.

As a result of social media, people live more publicly than ever before. The quality of their social life is judged on Instagram, their popularity on Snapchat, their career and achievements on LinkedIn.

There has also been some discussion that the parenting techniques of the baby boomers and Gen X, who sent mixed messages and both overpraised and criticised their 'trophy generation' offspring, have caused a greater propensity to feelings of inadequacy.

This can make millennials feel like they have something to prove and must validate their credentials, talent, attractiveness and social success. According to research for *TIME* magazine, this has led to many millennials feeling 'inadequate, overwhelmed and judged'.[28]

The anxieties that these imposter syndrome feelings create are usually completely, factually inaccurate, but they are real anxieties and need to be addressed to stop them preventing women from being able to speak up at all, or from speaking up confidently and advocating for themselves, their causes, their businesses.

These thoughts (whether consciously or, as is often the case, subconsciously) go a long way towards explaining why so many women choose not to take the risk of speaking, and why they can feel drained and debilitated by anxiety if they do push themselves to do it.

In summary, the princess paradigm and the imposter syndrome can lead women to:

- choose to not speak at all

- speak less

- wait longer to speak (sometimes missing the opportunity as a result)

- experience significant anxiety

I want to be clear at this point that identifying the impact of the princess paradigm is not about criticising women for some kind of 'bravery deficit'. The societal pressure is simply another barrier that gets in the way of women's progress.

Sandberg articulates this well in her book when she says 'I realised that in addition to institutional barriers, women face a battle from within'.[29] By recognising this and deploying strategies to counter it, women can both help themselves and call it out and campaign for the systemic changes that are required.

What to do

Here is how to deal with the need to be perfect and sense of inadequacy that stop you from speaking up confidently:

- be prepared to 'fail', meaning be prepared to not be perfect

- change the way you think

- CBT

- develop your skills

- develop your own style

- encourage and enable other women to speak

Be prepared to 'fail', ie be less than perfect

Many giants of their field have reached the pinnacle of success only by failing, learning and moving on. JK Rowling had her first Harry Potter manuscript rejected by 12 different publishers before one took it on. Most of the great inventors produced many products that didn't work until they finally came up with their breakthrough. The only English pope, Adrian IV, was rejected in his early attempts to become a monk at St Albans Abbey. Michael Jordan was dropped from his high school basketball team. Trying, failing and, importantly, learning and moving on are critical factors for success.

Women conforming to their ingrained conditioning to be perfect princesses and therefore not take risks and avoid the exposure of speaking up are losing vital opportunities for recognition and progress. You must:

- be bold

- ask for forgiveness, not permission

- be a warrior, not a worrier

- embrace trial and error as a learning curve

Change the way you think

Carol Dweck, in her book *Mindset*, characterises the fear of failure, permanent feeling of inadequacy and acceptance of your current limitations ('I am just not good at speaking') as what she defines as a fixed mindset. This, she suggests, is a harmful and limiting way of thinking. She advocates instead a growth mindset, a conscious decision to adopt a way of thinking that says: 'Well that presentation/speech/meeting didn't go so well, but never mind, I learned a lot from that and next time I need to do… and I will be better.'[30]

Susan Jeffers' book *Feel the Fear and Do it Anyway* suggests a similar thing, namely that pushing yourself out of your comfort zone is key to progress and to achieving both your speaking and life potentials.[31]

If, having understood from this chapter the root of your aversion to risk and feelings of inadequacy when it comes to speaking, you could choose to take the Roosevelt view that you have 'nothing to fear but fear itself'. That would help you feel OK about volunteering to speak, speaking up in meetings and persisting when you find it hard to be heard.

> Whatever you think you can do or
> believe you can do, begin it.
> *Action* has magic, grace and power in it.

Goethe, *Faust Part One*

CBT

Cognitive behavioural therapy has something to offer by way of a structured approach to challenging and changing the way you think. It suggests that the way we think determines how we feel, which in turn determines what we do and drives our behaviours.

Thoughts:

- I am not good at speaking
- I will make a fool of myself
- I will ruin my reputation/expose myself as a fraud

Lead to **feelings** of:

- inadequacy/I am not perfect
- embarrassment
- fear

Which leads to **behaviours** like:

- avoiding speaking
- speaking tentatively
- keeping quiet

Mammals are driven exclusively by how they feel, by their limbic system. The limbic system is common to mammals and humans and is our basic survival mechanism. It has no language, it just drives how we feel – safe or threatened – and how we react to keep safe. Humans, however, have a neo-cortex, the rational, logical part of the brain that allows conscious thought. It enables us to override instinctive reactions. This means that we can choose our thoughts. Instinctive, reactive thoughts will come to us (eg 'I am terrified. What am I doing on this stage?'), but what humans can do that mammals cannot is make a conscious decision to change our thoughts and produce different feelings and behaviours in ourselves.

Thoughts:

- I have the potential to be very good at speaking

- I will showcase my ideas and opinions

- I will build my reputation and my career

Lead to **feelings** of:

- curiosity to learn

- commitment to improve

- excitement

Which leads to **behaviours** like:

- developing speaking skills

- seeking opportunities to speak and contribute regularly

- speaking confidently with conviction

When you come across the opportunity to speak in public and your instinct kicks in and makes you want to only speak when you're 100% ready or not at all, ask yourself these two questions:

- What am I thinking?

- How is that making me feel?

If the answer is negative feelings that are inhibiting you, consider changing the thoughts to something more helpful.

Develop your skills

Don't try to be perfect, but do learn and develop your skills. Speaking is a disproportionately important skill and an enabling, gateway skill for so many things that any woman wants to achieve. It should never be downplayed or disregarded. Like many things in life, the more you practise, the easier it gets.

- Always seek feedback

- Always prepare well so you can ask questions in meetings and Q&As

- Take every speaking course you can

- Join Toastmasters (https://www.toastmasters.org/) or the Association of Speakers Club (https://www. the-asc.org.uk/) for practice

- Get a speaking coach for the biggest speaking events you have to participate in

- And here is the commercial break... contact me at: enquiries@archimedesconsulting.co.uk for coaching and support!

Encourage and enable other women to speak

Male or female, if you are a manager, teacher, trainer, medical consultant, training junior doctor or lecturer you have a role to play. Don't always simply throw questions out there and wait for the most confident and assertive (most often men) to reply.

I have probably led hundreds of workshops over my career and will confess I have been guilty of throwing questions out to the whole group, usually a mixed group. I always found the most confident men responded first. I now very consciously ask a mix of whole-group questions and specific individual questions.

By addressing questions to specific individuals, you give women an equal voice, and when called upon, women have plenty to say and usually express themselves confidently. You are also ensuring they are heard and not interrupted and overridden by anyone (often men). By doing this, you will get higher participation and more varied views.

CHAPTER 4

The Likeability Paradox

When conducting workshops with groups, I sometimes get them to play a word association game. You know the one, where I say a word and you write down whatever words first come into your mind.

When I ask for leadership characteristics, I get words like strong, powerful, decisive, determined, assertive, aggressive, forceful, competitive, visionary, inspiring, winner, brave. When I do the same word association exercise with male characteristics, this time it's remarkably similar, I get words like strong, decisive, determined, assertive, aggressive, competitive, winner, brave, bold.

Few surprises here. The paradigms of a historically male-dominated world will of course have ingrained concepts of leadership that are to do with power, risk taking and strength. The huge correlation between traditionally male traits and leadership traits is therefore to be expected. We need to look no further than some big names in politics and industry, such as Jack Welsh, Lee Iacocca, Rockefeller, Winston Churchill and Richard Branson to see that.

Finally, I ask what words spring to mind when we look at typical female characteristics. Words like gentle, nurturing, caring, collaborative, kind, accommodating, empathic and supportive are used.

So here's the crux of the problem: a woman displaying what society thinks of as typical leadership traits may be ticking the boxes of what we want from a leader, but she is also contravening all the societal norms of what we want, expect and, perhaps, demand from a woman.

New Zealand's female Prime Minister, Jacinda Ardern, summarised this well when she said: 'One of the criticisms I've faced over the years is that I'm not aggressive enough or assertive enough, or maybe somehow, because I'm empathetic, I'm weak.'

This double bind is called out when we think of the double standards often used to describe women as opposed to men. The same behaviours are often perceived and labelled differently depending on who is talking!

- A woman is bossy / a man has leadership skills

- A woman is aggressive / a man is assertive

- A woman is nagging / a man is persistent

- A woman is stubborn / a man is determined

- A woman is hysterical / a man is passionate

- A woman is pushy / a man is ambitious

To develop your career, to stand out, to be successful, to be heard, you have to speak out. To be a leader or leadership material, you have to be visible, determined and demonstrably confident, but when women behave like this, they are often judged negatively for it. When they speak up powerfully, when they articulate views and ideas that are strong and assertive, when they talk confidently about their achievements, they risk actually being *perceived* as less 'likeable'. Women face this double bind whenever they speak publicly.

The data clearly shows that men can be both liked and respected, whereas a professional woman can be one or the other and will find it much harder, if not impossible, to achieve both. Why is this?

The reason is something called prescriptive bias, which is how we expect people to behave. As the word association exercise regularly proves, societal and cultural expectations of men and women are very different and traits typically associated with a 'good woman' do not correlate closely with leadership. It is a form of unconscious bias, meaning that it is not an active, calculated form of judgment or discrimination.

When women display leadership traits, for many it feels unnatural and somehow wrong. Therefore, it is rejected at a subconscious level. End result? People then judge the women as not likeable. These norms may be unhelpful and anachronistic, but they are still deeply ingrained in our culture. Interestingly, it can be other, often older women who are most subconsciously offended by this variance from the norms that they themselves have lived by.

Much has been written about the queen bee syndrome, which describes a lone woman who has somehow navigated the issues, succeeded at the career game of snakes and ladders, made it to the top of her business or political organisation and then has effectively 'pulled up the ladder' behind her. The queen bee then declines to help or support other women, revelling in her unique situation as a woman among men. Margaret Thatcher was certainly accused of this.

Madeleine Albright, the first ever female US Secretary of State, said: 'There is a special place in hell for women who do not support other women.' There is an alternative view expressed by one woman I interviewed who said: 'Maybe they've just had such a hard time getting there, they are just trying to survive.'

Sheryl Sandberg, in her book *Lean In*, cites an experiment conducted at Columbia Business School and New York University by professors Frank Flynn and Cameron Anderson, respectively. They selected the CV of a real-life female entrepreneur, who was quite successful and noted for her extroverted personality. Her name was Heidi Rosen, so the name Heidi was placed on one of a set of identical CVs, and a man's name, Howard, on the other. Half of a group of business school students read one CV, and the other half the other.

The result was remarkable: the students rated Heidi and Howard as equally competent. However, Howard was judged to be likeable and a good colleague while Heidi was seen as aggressive, selfish and not someone who would be a team player or whom they would like to work with. Essentially, they found her less likeable.[32]

In the UK, a similar case study was conducted in which respondents were given the performance evaluation of a vet. Some participants were given the evaluation in which the vet being assessed was called Mark and the others were given one on which the name (and only the name) had been changed to Elizabeth.

Forty-four per cent rated Mark as significantly more competent than Elizabeth. They also felt that Mark should be paid significantly more. This demonstrates the inherent internal bias that people carry about typical gender roles and behaviours, and how men and women are judged by different rules, even when they are equally competent.

The importance of being liked

But do you need to be liked? Is it important to be liked to be a) effective in your role, and b) personally happy? Of course, everyone likes to be liked, but for some it is more important than for others. Typically, if you are an extrovert who draws energy and motivation from others, the need to be liked is likely to be higher in you than in a more introverted, internally motivated person. However, whatever your personality, you do need others to like you in order to be effective.

It is much harder to influence people if they don't like you. Robert Cialdini, who wrote a seminal book on influencing, lists 'liking' as one of the seven keys to influencing others.[33] Building a rapport, getting in synch with others, having them feel they warm to you, is critical in order for them to be open to what you have to say.

In politics, a rational policy platform and operational competence are not enough to get people to vote for you.

They also have to like you. As a political baroness once said to aspiring candidates: 'You've got to be the sort of person they want to go to the pub with after a day's campaigning.'

Hillary Clinton clearly suffered from this likeability double bind in her 2016 election loss to Donald Trump. She was probably one of the most qualified candidates to ever run for President of the US, given all her previous roles and experience. Yet, there was a marked trend of people, even former democrats, saying they couldn't vote for her because 'I just don't like her.' Clinton discusses this in her book *What Happened.*

Elaine Kamarck, a Senior Fellow at the Brookings Institution who served in Bill Clinton's administration, said: 'This business of people "not liking" her is shaped by expectations, by television, by what we think people in authority ought to look like, and not who she actually is.'

Interviews and selections

In terms of recruitment, selection and promotion, in an ideal world these processes should not be gender biased, but they are.

The double bind is particularly challenging for millennial women who are putting themselves forward for promotion, perhaps for the first time in their careers. In an interview situation in business or a selection meeting in a political sphere, of course you have to articulate the case strongly for how good you are and how high your potential is for the role in question. You have to sound confident in your abilities and achievements. And yet, when you do, the likability bias in the audience of your assessors or selectors can kick in and you can be perceived as being aggressive, cold, unfriendly or bragging (because, of course, societal norms expect women to be gentle and self-effacing). Talk about a lose-lose situation!

This is a recognised phenomenon and many organisations are trying to combat it with non-gender-specific selection processes, such as when the proportion of women in US orchestras, led by the Boston Philharmonic, went from 10% in the 1970s to 35% by the mid-1990s as a result of introducing blind auditions. CVs without names have also been introduced in some organisations but, of course, many, many roles still require your physical presence as part of the selection procedure and so likeability bias remains an issue.

One woman I interviewed was a country manager of a major multi-national food business. She told me that she was up for a prestigious award that was a really big deal in her company. She was on a shortlist of three (two men and her) and had to make a presentation to the global CEO as the final interview for the award. She was given a (male) coach to help her prepare for the presentation. The coach advised her that in presenting her and her team's work, she used 'us' and 'we' far too much. She was too self-effacing and needed to talk more about her achievements and instead use 'I' and 'me' to make it clear why she deserved the award. It was against the grain of what she would normally do, but she took the coach's advice.

Sadly, she did not win the award and the CEO gave the feedback afterwards that he did not like the way she had not given any credit to her team! The irony is that had the male coach been giving advice to a male presenter, it would have probably been right. For this female presenter, it was entirely wrong, and she was judged negatively for being as bullish and self-promoting as the men.

A second interviewee, a senior executive in the insurance industry, also told me that she was being coached by male mentors to be more assertive, 'sharper-elbowed' and to put herself first in what she did and how she articulated herself. She did as she had been told when requesting a pay increase upon being asked to take on a wider role with more responsibility: she expressed herself forcefully and kept pressing hard. Her reward was to be taken aside by a board member and told to stop, as she was annoying people!

In summary, the likeability double bind can:

- cause women to instinctively understand this likeability penalty, fear being disliked and therefore feel less inclined to speak up

- cause women to routinely and significantly self-edit, always feeling the need to soften what they say and how they say it, which is exhausting

- mean that when you speak, you struggle to feel 'heard' or taken seriously, or that you experience feeling dismissed

- lead to frustration and even anger at feeling 'damned if you do, damned if you don't', which in turn can lead you to become combative in the way you speak and bring down yet more negative judgment upon you

What to do

How do women position themselves to be strong, successful, competent, and yet likeable when giving speeches or presentations, in interviews or in meetings?

Navigate

- strike a balance – walk the tightrope

- build relationships – with individuals and the audience

Challenge

- call it out

- humour

- establish a new paradigm

- be a difficult woman

Strike a balance

In an interview situation, for example, say enough about your background to ensure people know that you are credible and successful, but be wary of saying too much about your achievements. A long list of 'and then I did…' may not be the most effective approach.

Women's natural tendencies can cause many of us to not want to brag about what we've accomplished, but when it comes to interviews and selections we know we have to talk more about ourselves and our achievements. As a result, we push ourselves out of our comfort zones and can end up coming across as too forced, unnatural or too 'pushy' in articulating what we have achieved.

Finding a way to strike a good balance and practising how we position our career and CV details are key skills for women. One approach is to use stories or anecdotes and wrap your achievements and experience into that, eg 'I feel strongly about that issue, I found that when I was leading the project on the acquisition, we had to adapt our strategy to…'

Build relationships

Traditionally, the way successful women have overcome the likeability issue is to work harder, much harder, at business relationships. Whereas a man could get away with walking past his PA's desk, dropping a report on it and saying straightforwardly: 'Can I have this for Monday, please?', the equivalent behaviour in a woman would be considered brusque, abrupt and uncaring. She may even be considered 'a b*tch'.

Instead the dialogue would probably go something like 'Hi, how was your weekend/game/kid?' and after a suitable length of exchange: 'I really need this for Monday, I'd be really grateful if you could have it for me by then.' Clearly, this is time-consuming but as a communication style it meets the expectations of being a female (caring, gentle, etc) while still requesting the task and getting it done in the time required.

I asked former Home Secretary Amber Rudd how she was able to deal with the likeability issue. She said it was partly because she was prepared to take risks and partly because she had other options than being a politician. More importantly, she said she would always go out of her way to take people aside, recognise and thank them and make sure they were aware of how important they were to her and to achieving departmental objectives. She said: 'I definitely worked harder at relationships than my male counterparts.'

As a way to communicate, spending time on relationships is probably something men should do more of and not women less of!

In speeches and presentations, you can still build relationships with your audience. First, you need to get to know your audience. Then, you can build audience-centric presentations around what THEY want to hear (not what YOU want to tell them).

Try to insert comments that are positive and complimentary about your audience collectively. You can do this via research and being well informed and up-to-date on what is happening in the group, their local area, their business, their department.

Recognising, acknowledging or thanking specific individuals in the audience can also be a way to build relationships.

This clearly has to be done subtly and authentically, where there is actual cause for praise for example, otherwise you risk appearing to be 'sucking up'. For example, saying you are delighted to be there when you are in the middle of nowhere might lack a ring of authenticity!

Getting this wrong is a guaranteed way to break the relationship with the audience and end up in the middle of the likability swamp. I went to a presentation at my daughters' school (a girls' school) for a parental briefing on university applications. The speaker started giving us a hard sell on reasons to go to university – the parents and kids there had already decided to apply! She was clearly recycling a standard presentation and then, by repeatedly saying 'your sons and daughters'(!) she lost me and most of the audience. The speaker's likeability and competence scores with that audience hit the floor.

Call it out

There is an ancient Greek rhetorical device called 'refutation'. What you do is outline the issue or objection that you face, clearly and openly. You bring into the open what people may be thinking (consciously or even subconsciously), which then enables you to offer the counter argument. In an interview or selection presentation, this might sound like 'I've done x, y, z in my career and achieved a, b, c. Now, some people might think that makes me aggressive and hyper competitive, which of course is not what we might expect women to be. I am sure, however, that you are more sophisticated than that and do not buy into those anachronistic stereotypes of women. Yes, I work hard, and yes, I compete to win, but that makes me someone who strives constantly for the good of my employees / my company / my objectives and that's what I am doing / would do for you.'

Humour

Humour is a double-edged sword in terms of speaking. It can be an incredibly powerful tool. It can diffuse hostility and prejudice and lighten tough topics, and it can enable women to speak forcefully without being seen as aggressive. I heard one black, female, prospective parliamentary candidate who started her speech at a selection meeting in a leafy, rural constituency with the line: 'I'm glad to be here in X and I could tell you that my family has been here since the Norman conquest, but I guess that wouldn't work well!' It raised a good laugh, it worked as a subtle refutation against any racial prejudice and got her off to a good start. She was selected and is now the local MP.

Humour certainly does not need to mean cracking jokes or trying to be a comedienne like Miranda, but good one-liners or humorous stories can definitely help with likeability. The caveat is that it can be risky. If humour falls flat it can kill a speech or presentation and an ill-judged, off-the-cuff humorous comment in meetings or Q&A sessions can misfire badly.

My rule of thumb is if you tend to tell stories and use one-liners in the way you normally talk, then they definitely could be a good defence against likability issues. If that's not normally your style, then do not use this to kick off a high-stake presentation or meeting.

Establish a new paradigm

Given that the vast majority of senior leaders are men (as are the leaders of FTSE 100 companies), the cultural and social paradigm of men as leaders is still strong.

Be wary of advice from male mentors and coaches to be 'more assertive', 'stronger' and more self-promoting. That is advice that may well work for other men, but not for women. The Henry Higgins-style advice ('why can't a woman be more like a man?') is very likely to be counterproductive for women and to cause them to run headlong into that glass wall / ceiling and to fight unsuccessfully against the likeability bias. The key is to develop your own style and be confident in it.

After the tragic shooting incident in New Zealand in 2019 (where a gunman killed over 50 worshippers at a mosque), the female Prime Minister of New Zealand, Jacinda Ardern, demonstrated that leadership and being a politician can look different from the traditional male-orientated paradigms.

She took strong and assertive action in rapidly driving through much tougher gun controls and committing government resources and money to support the bereaved families. She also communicated female traits of gentleness and compassion in how she hugged and comforted the survivors. Given the dramatic circumstances, the whole world noticed this and applauded this model of leadership.

No one suggested that she was weak for showing active empathy or that she was unfeminine for taking assertive action on gun law change.

When you speak, have the confidence to be yourself and bring that great female mix of skills to the party. Bring that blend of compassion, empathy, nurture and care with strength, assertiveness and drive, and demonstrate what a powerful package that it is.

Be a difficult woman

If you do not think it is right to adapt to the demands of the current societal norms, and you are willing to challenge, then you may have to make your peace with being more respected than liked – to, perhaps, be a 'bloody difficult woman', as Ken Clarke once called former Prime Minister Theresa May.

To an extent, Theresa May turned it around by taking the intended criticism and wearing it as a badge of honour, including the phrase in her speeches and making something of a joke of it. 'Bloody Difficult Woman' T-shirts are now widely available!

CHAPTER 5

The critic and the troll

'I have found the perfect target. This c*** needs to feel our full wrath. Are you up for it? Are you prepared to take her down?' 'Find her children and make their life a living hell.'

When women speak up and speak out, they risk vitriolic criticism and abuse. The quotes above are examples of what Caitlin Roper, a UK journalist, found when she started researching her critics. These are shocking and extreme, but they illustrate a hugely widespread phenomenon.

Criticism and abuse do form a barrier to women speaking. It taps into some of our deep-rooted evolutionary fears of ostracism. Human beings are essentially social creatures;

when we were cavemen and cavewomen we needed to stay in groups for safety and security in order to survive against the wider environment of threats from sabre-toothed tigers and opposing tribes. Being ostracised, being cast out, being sent 'beyond the pale', was effectively a death sentence.

In our 21st century human manifestations, we still feel that fear of being cast out. Ask any teenage girl being 'aired' by her friendship group, you will find her stress and anxiety as real as ever. Being unfairly criticised and abused taps into our fear of being outside our group, our workplace, our colleagues, our community or geography. If speaking out poses all of these risks, it logically follows that keeping quiet is a better, safer option. For women to speak in public, they then have to push themselves way out of their comfort zone.

There is neurological research that suggests women are more susceptible to criticism than men because women process emotional energy differently, are typically more emotionally intelligent and hence more aware of, and sensitive to, criticism. So, not only they are more criticised, but they feel the impact more acutely.

Some would argue (note the refutation) that criticism and abuse of high-profile female journalists, politicians and public figures is one thing, but that criticism in the workplace is fair and to be expected by women in business

– surely it is part of learning and developing and women cannot expect special treatment and ask not to be criticised because they're 'delicate little flowers'.

That is far, far from the case! Professional people – men and women – expect and, if they're smart, welcome constructive criticism. It is indeed the way you learn and grow, but that is not what I am talking about here.

Abuse

Women are criticised more often and more personally than men and often in a way that is demeaning and abusive.

During the 2017 UK general election, Amnesty International did an analysis of the critical or abusive tweets received by female MPs. In a five-month period there were 25,668 abusive tweets sent to female MPs.

There were 191 female MPs at the time. If we do the maths, this would translate into 134 abusive tweets per MP at the rate of 27 a month, or roughly one a day. In fact, one woman in particular received nearly half of all those tweets: Diane Abbott, MP was the shadow home secretary at the time and is the longest-serving and first ever black female MP. She was first elected in 1987. Her treatment does much to illustrate that whatever challenges women face in speaking up, women of colour face even more.[34]

Black women were 84% more likely to be mentioned in abusive or problematic tweets, according to Fix The Glitch.[35] It was depressing that 18 female MPs stood down at the 2019 election, most of them citing systematic abuse as one of their reasons for doing so. Sam Smethers, CEO of the Fawcett Society said: 'We have to confront the fact that our toxic politics is driving good women MPs away. In 2019 it is still a hostile environment for women.'

In the US, in July 2020, Congresswoman Alexandria Ocasio-Cortez delivered a powerful speech, castigating a fellow member of Congress for calling her a 'f***ing b*tch' on the steps of Capitol Hill. She said: 'These were the words he levied against a Congresswoman, the Congresswoman that not only represents New York's 14th Congressional District, but every Congresswoman and every woman in this country, because all of us have had to deal with this in some form, some way, some shape, at some point in our lives... This issue is not about one incident. It is cultural. It is a culture of... accepting violence and violent language against women, an entire structure of power that supports men.'[36]

Back in the UK, Caroline Criado-Perez was the target of extensive abuse when she spoke out in favour of having Jane Austen on the £10 banknote (so that there would not be only men on all UK banknotes). She received death and rape threats from 86 different Twitter accounts. Not for the first or (probably) last time, she was called a 'feminazi'.

The abuse women receive gets even more pernicious when it tips over from verbal abuse into actual violence. I know of a Conservative councillor in a Labour area of Liverpool who had a brick thrown through the window of her house where her baby was sleeping. Specific rape threats are often sent. The worst case scenario is the devastating murder of Jo Cox, the female MP for Batley and Spen, in 2016.

Microaggression

Away from the situations where violent, abusive language is used against them, women also suffer disproportionately from what is known as 'microaggressions' more than men. Microaggressions are a common occurrence in the workplace. They may consist of disparaging comments that vary from unfair criticism to having your judgment challenged or being overlooked for promotion.

Seventy-three per cent of women have experienced at least one type of microaggression. Sixteen per cent of women say they experience hearing demeaning remarks about 'people like you'. That figure rises significantly for women of colour, women with disabilities and women from the LGBTQ community.

The issue here is not that women are too soft to take a fair criticism or even the occasional unfair one. The issue is that these microaggressions, these routine, regular criticisms and disparagements have a grinding down effect, which can in turn silence women.

Disproportionate criticism

In *Invisible Women*, Caroline Criado-Perez talks about how women are typically judged much more harshly and criticised far more than men in performance assessments.[37] She quotes an analysis of 248 performance reviews collected from a range of US-based technology companies which found that women receive negative personality criticism that you don't see in men's reviews. Examples included 'bossy, abrasive, strident, aggressive, emotional and irrational'. Of all these words, only aggressive appeared in any of the male assessments, and that was to suggest more of it!

Women who do continue to speak up and speak out can feel like they face an uphill battle to be heard and be taken seriously. I recently spoke with a female CTO; she is the only woman on the board and said she was feeling like she struggled to get her colleagues to listen to her. Little wonder she became embattled and felt the need to be much more forceful (and therefore perceived as aggressive/ conflictual and accused of 'coming from a place of conflict, not communication')! She said the daily battle to be heard was making her role 'hard and lonely'.

Research from Yale[38] used a case study which demonstrated how women are criticised more than men. The case study gave groups of participants a fictional news story about a police chief in a major city preparing for a big protest rally. The protest got violent. In the story, the chief didn't send enough officers and 25 people were seriously injured. Different groups were given the same study, but some had a male police chief and others a female one.

Did it matter whether the police chief who made the bad call was male or female? It did. The male police chief saw his rating as an effective chief drop by roughly 10%. When a female police chief made the same mistake, her ratings dropped by almost 30%. Participants reading the story also wanted to demote her, but their counterparts did not want to demote him. Both leaders made a poor decision that backfired, but it cost her more.[6]

Personal criticism

When women are criticised, it is often very personal criticism that focusses not on the issues at hand or their achievements, views or competence, but on how they look and sound.

In 2017, two of the most senior figures in the UK, Prime Minister Theresa May and Scotland's First Minister Nicola Sturgeon, met to discuss Brexit. It was an issue of fundamental importance for the future of the UK, the European Union, jobs and the economy. The two women were pictured in smart business clothes, jackets and skirts. What was the headline in the *Daily Mail*? 'Never Mind Brexit, who won Legs-It'! I found it shocking that well into the 21st century a major national newspaper in the UK would, or could, publish a headline like this.

Helen Whatley, a government minister in the midst of the coronavirus crisis and lockdown in the UK, posted a picture of herself clapping outside her house at the regular Thursday 'Clap for our Carers'. The tweet said: 'Thank you to all those caring for the people we love.' One of the comments she got on Twitter was: 'Good God, you look like you've been through the mangle, why would you put this up and not expect criticism?' The premise being that unless you look great, you are fair game to be criticised, ignored and disparaged.

Lady Hale was head of the UK Supreme Court. She graduated top of her class in law at Cambridge. She is a professor of law, the first woman to be appointed to the Law Commission and the second to be appointed to the Court of Appeal. When she ruled against a government decision to prorogue Parliament, she was derided and criticised, not for her legal interpretation but for being the old woman with the crazy spider brooch.

And then there is Donald Trump. When thinking of examples of his overt misogyny, abuse and criticism of women it is difficult to know where to start. We could talk about his routinely calling Hillary Clinton 'that nasty woman', or we could discuss his quasi-official campaign slogan of 'Ditch the bitch.' 'Horse face', 'lowlife', 'fat', 'ugly' and 'a dog' are all words Trump has used publicly to talk about women. He described Arianna Huffington as 'ugly inside and out'.

Speechwriter Simon Lancaster pointed out that the 'bitch metaphor' has been used to keep women quiet since the 7th century BC when Semonides wrote about women as bitches, constantly barking. In ancient Roman times brothels were called 'lupanaria' (wolf dens). The public use of the word 'bitch' has trebled since the 1990s.

When referring to Gretchen Whitmer, the Democrat Governor of Michigan, with whom he disagreed about the extent of lockdown needed to keep people safe during the coronavirus crisis, Donald Trump called her 'Gretchen "Half" Whitmer' and said she was out of her depth. He was abusively belittling her, with no factual information about her policy or why he might disagree with it. At a White House press conference in 2020 he told one female reporter 'keep your voice down' and refused to answer her questions.

You could argue that Donald Trump is just an extraordinary aberration, but Republican Representative Ryan A. Costello accurately summarised the wider importance of his behaviour when he tweeted: 'To say this is unbecoming of any man, let alone the POTUS (President of the United States), is a vast understatement. And to say this enables teenage boys to feel they have a license to refer to girls with such names is obvious. It is all very embarrassing.'

I would argue it is more than simply embarrassing; it amplifies and justifies men and boys in feeling that it is OK to direct personal and unwarranted criticism at women. It normalises misogyny.

The spectrum of criticism women experience is wide and varies from mild, regular microaggressions to personal, appearance-based criticism, violent abusive language and, ultimately, actual violence. The cumulative effect of it all is to silence women.

Twitter's failure to adequately respect human rights and effectively tackle violence and abuse on the platform means that instead of women using their voices to impact the world, many women are instead being pushed backwards to a culture of silence.

Amnesty International[39]

On the occasion of the 31st anniversary of the founding of the World Wide Web, its inventor, Tim Berners-Lee, said:

'The dangerous trend in online abuse is forcing women out of jobs… silencing female opinions... the web is not working for women and girls.'

Why does this criticism and abuse happen? Many would argue this is the intention (consciously or subconsciously) of the criticism and abuse: to 'put women in their place', to keep them quiet, to keep the 4,000-year-old silence project going. Yet, of course, many, many women are not silenced. They continue to put themselves out there publicly to speak up for themselves, their ideas, their careers, their beliefs and their communities. But often at a cost to themselves, their wellbeing and their careers.

The culture of criticism and abuse:

- discourages women from speaking out, especially on controversial or political subjects

- increases women's anxiety about speaking

- makes it harder for women to be heard above the 'noise' and distraction of criticism

- legitimises unfounded personal criticism that makes it easier for women's thoughts and ideas to be dismissed

- makes women feel embattled and forces them to become more combative in how they speak

What to do

Navigate

- separate the personal and the professional
- ignore the criticism
- manage your 'state'
- handle the criticism

Challenge

- excel at Q&A
- learn to manage questions well
- report and prosecute

Separate the personal and professional

Arianna Huffington, founder of Huff Post, says that withstanding criticism is a critical skill for women and she realised early in her career that if she was going to speak out, she would always offend someone. She feels that it is not helpful to tell women to 'man up' and not care (or pretend not to). She advocates allowing yourself to feel the anger or hurt you experience, then consciously make a decision to move on and leave it behind.

When asked an aggressive question, especially one with implied or actual criticism embedded in it, or when we're directly criticised, it is easy to be offended or upset. Contemporary social media have encouraged people to criticise in a very harsh and personal-sounding way. In handling criticism, it is always good to remind yourself that it is not actually personal; the vast majority of the time the criticism is about the role, the job, the system, not the real human being (you) behind it.

Seema Kennedy, a former MP and minister, recounts the story of a lady vicar telling her that the critical or abusive people she encountered were usually targeting the dog collar, not her. Kennedy used to reassure herself by saying: 'I am more than my rosette.' Julia Gillard, former Prime Minister of Australia, said that you must have a strong sense of self, the real you, that you hold on to and actively defend in order to create a shield between the public you and the private one.

Ignore the criticism

One approach is to simply ignore illegitimate or offensive criticism to avoid giving oxygen to the critics and their negative points, thereby suffocating them – engaging with them and taking illegitimate criticism seriously can end up legitimising both.

This is certainly true for online criticism. There is a report published by the Center for Countering Digital Hate (CCDH) entitled *Don't feed the trolls*. Its premise is that on social media, especially Twitter, people feel freer to be more extreme and that is not the place for reasoned debate, therefore ignoring the 'trolls' is a good strategy. Fix The Glitch (www.fixtheglitch.org) is another organisation that can help women dealing with online abuse.

It is also possible to ignore verbal criticism in meetings or in the Q&A (questions and answers) section of a presentation or speech. The key here is to train yourself to not be triggered by the criticism, to discount it and listen for the point (assuming there is one!), and then specifically deal with the point – ignore the criticism. This is not always easy to do as we are often hurt or offended by the criticism and that distracts us and demands our attention. If, however, you can recognise what is happening and focus on the intellectual challenge of discerning a point, that can give you something to focus on beyond the criticism.

An example might be: 'Why do you think destroying people's livelihoods with these redundancies is acceptable?' You need to extract any valid question quickly, such as fear of redundancies, and address that, not the emotive criticism about destroying livelihoods. You might reply: 'The management's paramount concern is the welfare of its workforce, and whilst we never want redundancies, sometimes they are necessary to protect the wider workforce and the viability of the business.'

Manage your state

When confronted with illegitimate criticism we are not in a great place psychologically. It is worth learning to manage your own physiological state proactively, which will put you in a much more resourceful mindset to deal with the criticism.

When someone criticises us, it feels like a threat. Our brains have not really evolved that much over the past 100,000 years, so the sense of threat we feel from even a relatively mild criticism can be interpreted as life-threatening by our brains, equivalent to a confrontation with the sabre-toothed tiger I mentioned earlier in the chapter.

To our caveman brain, criticism and verbal abuse trigger all of our automated survival instincts. Our limbic system, the primeval, mammalian part of our brain, automatically responds and puts our body in a state of high alert to deal with the impending threat. Our body floods with stress hormones and, at a visceral level, we are in full-on fight-or-flight mode. When our brain and body flood with stress hormones such as adrenaline and cortisol, it is physiologically hard to think straight, as those hormones incapacitate the rational, logical parts of our brain (at least for a while). It therefore becomes harder to respond well to the challenge. In his book *Emotional Intelligence*, Daniel Goleman describes this as an emotional hijack.[40]

Recognising that your limbic system has been triggered is the first step towards allowing the emotional part of your brain to drain itself of the stress hormone and the logical part of your brain to take over and start processing a response. Breathing helps! When we're stressed, we take short, sharp breaths and our bodies feel deprived of air and feel even more threatened – this is what happens when people have a panic attack. Take in some oxygen, breathe deeply from your diaphragm. This allows your body to start relaxing, enabling you to come out of fight-or-flight mode and start thinking logically to process a response.

This fight-or-flight state is, of course, made much worse if we are already at a physically low ebb because we are tired, hungry or not properly hydrated. Ensuring you take care of yourself before going into a potentially stressful situation is critical for making you feel balanced, grounded and able to take on a challenge.

Handle the criticism

Develop a series of techniques and phrases that can be part of your criticism 'toolkit':

- reflect back
- use humour
- name the criticism
- ask for evidence / data
- ask critics to explain the point of their criticism

Reflect back

You can seek to diffuse the criticism by showing some understanding of (but not agreement with) the other person's issue or position, for example: 'I'm sorry you clearly feel upset / offended / frustrated, etc by this, but allow me to address your concern…'

Use humour

You can deflect criticism with humour. Oscar Wilde's retort 'I refuse to have a battle of wits with an unarmed person' is a favourite of mine. Humour can work; however, it can also be perceived as a counterattack and can further incense a critic (particularly one with a sensitive male ego) rather than diffuse the situation. Use humour with caution.

Name the criticism

One tactic when someone is criticising you unfairly is to identify the specific criticism and call it out. You could say something like: 'So, you're saying you think I'm doing a poor job?' When critics are confronted with a clear restatement of their veiled or implied criticism, they will often back down. Even if they do not, you've brought it out in the open and can clearly offer the counter-argument. This can work particularly well when the premise of their criticism is clearly flawed. Using the previous example, you could say: 'So, you are saying that you think my intention is to destroy livelihoods?'

Ask for evidence / data

If you know the criticism is unfounded, then asking the critic to justify or validate it can work well, using questions like: 'On what basis do you say that?' or 'What information / data / evidence do you have to substantiate that claim?'

Ask them to explain the point of their criticism

If someone is criticising you or other women unfairly or personally rather than professionally, you should call it out. You could say: 'What's that got to do with the issue at hand?' 'Could you explain the link? I can't see how my / her appearance / voice is relevant here.' or 'Would you have asked this if I / she were a man?' Calling out unfounded criticism of other women is certainly something you should do if you are keen to fix the system.

The effectiveness of these challenges or push-backs is all about tone and delivery. You can convey some direct messages and make strong challenges without being hated if you do it in an even tone that is neither defensive nor aggressive.

Excel at Q&A

If you think you are going to face criticism in a meeting or presentation, preparation is vital. As they say in the military: train hard, fight easy. Forewarned is forearmed.

Even if you don't expect to get any criticism or opposition, you should spend some time thinking about your audience and the following questions:

- What are the three worst questions I could be asked?

- Who is not going to like this?

- What will their criticisms be (both legitimate and illegitimate)?

- What angle are they going to come from?

If you brainstorm likely questions and criticisms (both straightforward and tricky ones) and plan out rough answers, it will help you feel prepared to handle them and any possible variations. When dealing with a known challenging issue, get a clear idea of what you want to achieve: do you want to listen? propose? inform? Knowing that will give you a clearer approach.

You should also prepare your red lines. What are you not prepared to discuss? What criticism are you not prepared to engage with, and do you plan to ignore it or challenge it? Knowing this in advance means you are much better prepared and will not need to come up with responses while managing your emotions.

Question management

You don't have to be at the mercy of the audience's questions and criticisms. It pays to take control of the logistics and manage the audience's expectations, especially if you anticipate some criticism, or challenging or hostile questions.

- You can specify how you plan to handle questions:

    o you can, for example, state at the start of your presentation that you will only take questions at the end of your speech; that is often enough to stop people trying to interrupt with questions

    o you can also ask for questions to be submitted via a chairman/ chairwoman (if you have one), which may give you more time to think and formulate your response

    o you can ask for written questions, which minimises the impact of less concise questioners and insulates you from the aggressive ones

- A frequently used approach is to take three or more questions at a time. This enables you to focus on the one you really want to answer and handle the other two, which may contain the personal or unfair criticism, in much less detail.

- If you are really put on the spot, writing down the question can help you process it.

- If the person asking the question is talking for a long time you can also start jotting down bullet points of content for your response. Asking for clarification, eg: 'I want to address your concern, but I am unclear on your question, could you expand on what you mean by X?' also buys you time to think.

- Finally, you should not be afraid to admit to something you don't know; no one's omnipotent but promising to get back to the questioner with a response (and doing so) is a fair response to that circumstance.

Facing stormy or critical speaking situations is rarely going to be something you relish! However, like so many things, you just need to learn and practise some useful techniques and approaches.

Report and prosecute

Finally, challenge and confront criticism of an excessive, abusive or threatening nature whenever possible. Get the authorities involved, whether that is by reporting abuse to the relevant platform, eg Facebook or Twitter, or getting HR, or even the police, involved. Fix The Glitch (fixtheglitch.org) is an organisation that supports women against online abuse. It has tools and resources on its website including, for example, a form that allows you to collect relevant information you need to report abuse.

Jess Phillips is an outspoken Labour MP who gets much abuse. She says that is one of the hardest things, and death and rape threats do have to be taken seriously and are immensely time consuming, 'There's a big process you have to go through with the police and house authorities and extra security needed.'

It may be hard work, but it is necessary for your own protection and also to hold the critics and abusers to account, to make them think twice before subjecting you and other women to such abuse.

Notes

You can use this space to make specific notes on your application of the ideas or techniques mentioned above.

PART 2

SKILL

Part 1 has been about understanding and recognising some of the social norms, stereotypes and paradigms that affect women and their willingness to speak and ability to be heard.

Part 2 looks at specific areas of speaking in public and how millennial women can maximise their effectiveness in these areas.

By understanding some of these phenomena earlier in your career, you can accelerate your progress towards your goals.

CHAPTER 6

Language

The language we use not only reflects our culture but constructs it.

Aurélie Salvaire, *Balance the World*

Language matters. I want to look at it in two ways:

1. language used by women themselves in the current culture that undermines their message

2. language used in talking about women that prevents their being 'heard', acknowledged and accepted

Do women use language differently from men?

In the mid-70s, linguist Robin Lakoff wrote an essay called *Language and Woman's Place*. She proposed the idea that women use language differently from men, and that their usage both reflects and perpetuates their subordinate status. She suggested that women use plenty of qualifiers and minimisers, as well as gentle, soft words and avoid slang and swear words and phrases so as not to sound too 'strident' and 'unfeminine'.[41]

In the 80s and 90s there was a popular book, *Men are from Mars and Women are from Venus*.[42]

It essentially suggested that the reason men and women often have difficulty understanding each other is because they inherently speak a different language, and that if you understood those different languages, you could communicate better. It spawned almost an entire genre of books on the same theme.

More recent research has shown that, in fact, these earlier ideas were not so much founded on research as on the author's thoughts or ideas.

Linguist Deborah Cameron recently published a book called *The Myth of Mars and Venus* in which she contends that data, rather than what she describes as 'soundbite science', actually shows that there are few inherent differences in how men and women use language, and what differences there are are the result of the evolution of society and the changing nature of men's and women's roles.

Cameron writes: 'Culture change is inherently hard: it causes anxiety, conflict and in some quarters resistance.' She says that the challenges of change cause people to want simplistic solutions that enable them to sigh and say 'Well, that's just the way men are, or women are.'[43]

Although language is not about inherent differences between men and women, language, and how we use it, does tell us a lot about how women and men still see their roles and how societal paradigms still 'expect' us to behave.

Language used against women

Language tends to reflect the cultural paradigm that men are the default human beings and women are the exception. Gendered words like 'policeman', 'fireman', 'chairman', etc reflect the fact that these roles were traditionally exclusive male preserves, while non-gendered terms like 'police officer', 'firefighter' or 'chair' are being adopted very slowly, illustrating the glacial pace of change of societal paradigms.

Using language that excludes, marginalises or demeans women perpetuates the ancient stereotypes that continue to hold women back and makes it hard for them to speak and be heard.

There are many demeaning or derogatory terms used to describe women or female behaviour that do not really have male equivalents: phrases like 'ice queen', 'highly strung', 'time of the month', 'catfight'.

Men are rarely described by their hair colour – 'he's a blonde / brunette / redhead' is not a phrase I have ever heard! Yet women are often described by some element of their appearance, as if that is their defining feature. When challenged, some men will dismiss female concerns with this type of language, calling it petty or symptomatic of militant feminism rather than just a fair desire not to be belittled. After Donald Trump was infamously caught in 2016 telling a reporter that it was OK to 'grab women by the pussy', he dismissed the subsequent criticism by saying it was 'just locker-room talk'.

Even casual or inadvertent use of language can often reveal inherent assumptions about the ascendancy of men in powerful roles and make women feel on the outside edges. In May 2020, *The Daily Telegraph* ran a story about the potential issues of MPs voting remotely as they had to do during the pandemic crisis. The headline read: 'Wives, researchers or children could be voting for MPs'. The underlying premise was that MPs are heterosexual males with wives.

Female MP Jess Phillips called this out by tweeting: 'Well, I'll have to make sure my wife doesn't vote then!' *The Daily Telegraph* quickly capitulated and changed its headline to 'spouses' instead. This small example is symptomatic of how assumptions about women's traditional roles are baked into language used day in, day out.[44]

Sometimes the language used to marginalise women is very subtle. Suggesting that something is 'little', 'small', 'young' or 'cute' can diminish the relevance or value of women's comments, roles or credibility.

During the COVID-19 crisis, when talking about Gretchen Whitmer, the Democrat Governor of Michigan with whom he disagreed about the extent of lockdown needed to keep people safe, President Trump said he had a big problem with 'the young woman governor' (she was 49 at the time!).

Have you ever told someone about your new project or perhaps a recent award you had received, only to be told 'Oh great, that's that little project on…' or 'Oh, that's so cute'?

All of these are examples of language that can create an environment that causes women to feel like outsiders and embattled, which in turn can cause them to either remain silent or feel like they have to be overassertive to be heard.

Tone policing

'Tone policing' refers to men who try to tell women what their language and tone should and should not be. This can include criticising women for sounding aggressive (usually meaning 'speaking directly') or telling a female reporter to 'keep her voice down' as Donald Trump did. It also includes situations like UK government minister Matt Hancock telling MP Rosena Allin-Khan she 'might do well to take a leaf out of the Shadow Secretary of State's book in terms of tone.'

These are all examples of men telling women what is and is not appropriate language and tone for them to use. Failure to conform to the expected norms usually results in women being criticised and described in negative terms (eg 'shrew', 'harpy'), and even abused.

Use of language that impedes women

Primacy and recency

When you're doing a presentation or speech, people mostly only remember the first and last things you say. This means that the first thing you say is pivotal to how your audience perceives you. Using precise language, choosing words well and rehearsing are vital.

If you don't have time for anything else, ensuring you get the language and delivery right at the beginning and at the end is critical. It sets the scene for the rest of what you have to say. I have seen countless presentations start with something like: 'Well, er… sorry, I didn't really have much time to prepare this' or 'I'm not very good at this sort of thing, but here goes.' Equally, I've heard far too many presentations tail off at the end with something like 'and that's it, that's all I've got, really' or 'and, er… yeah.'

Unfortunately, women tend to use these types of beginning and ending more often than men, who tend to brazen it out, whereas women have a tendency to be more open and use language that reflects their nervousness.

Self-effacing and self-deprecating comments

'I'm no expert…' 'I am sure that others would know better than me...' 'It's perhaps not that interesting, but…' 'It was nothing really, just doing my job...' 'It was just a small project...'

Women are often quick to make self-effacing comments. There are times when they are relevant and useful. If you are very powerful or very senior, then being seen as self-effacing can signal humility and self-depreciation. It can be a humorous counterpoint to your position of power.

In most speaking situations, however, self-effacing comments undermine your power and credibility: you are effectively telling your audience you're not to be trusted or taken seriously.

Given the evidence presented in previous chapters of how societal norms are slow to accord women status and credibility, such comments are particularly damaging to women's credibility. The definition and synonyms of 'self-effacing' shed light on why women do this more than men.

The definition of self-effacing is 'having or showing a tendency to make oneself modestly or shyly inconspicuous'. 'To efface' means 'to erase', so self-effacing or deprecating comments are used when trying to be invisible, to lower one's profile, to keep one's head below the parapet to avoid being shot at.

The synonyms for self-effacing are also interesting: 'bashful', 'coy', 'demure', 'modest', 'retiring' – all words that relate closely to traditional feminine virtues. Women are still lauded for displaying these characteristics and judged negatively for not displaying them, so it is not surprising that using self-effacing language can feel good and 'right' for women.

One woman I interviewed, who worked in corporate banking in the 80s, was told early in her career not to use language that would make men feel challenged, but to use this kind of self-effacing language instead. She said: 'In the beginning of my professional career, I was advised by both men and women to be non-confrontational and show deference before speaking up, particularly in group meetings – this often sounded like "maybe I'm wrong... maybe something to consider... I'm no expert, but..." Unfortunately, this seemed to reinforce that I didn't have the credibility to speak and weakened my points substantially.'

You would have hoped that this need for deference went out with 80s shoulder pads and is no longer there for millennial women, any more than the need for self-deprecating comments. However, in 2018, participants in an EY women's development programme were being given almost exactly this same advice. The course materials stated: 'You have to offer your thoughts in a benign way.' This goes to prove this societal norm it is still there, (albeit subtly) and subconsciously affecting the language women use.

Qualifiers and minimisers

We all, men and women, have our little vocal tics and 'go-to' words we habitually use to punctuate our speech and pad out what we say when we're unsure or nervous about a topic. In the same way that self-effacing language hurts women more than men, some of these filler words can undermine a woman's message when she speaks or presents.

Qualifiers are words and phrases like 'sort of', 'kind of', 'maybe', 'perhaps' or 'might'. They are equivocations, often used to soften our message when we are worried about delivering a tough message, being perceived as too pushy or aggressive, or about people not liking our message.

These words are then used as a defensive mechanism to save the speaker from being criticised or disliked. This is mainly a subconscious process: people often do not realise they are doing it. While both men and women use qualifiers, women are particularly prone to it to try and avoid being judged as 'strident' or 'unfeminine'. The issue, however, is that the speaker usually ends up sounding tentative and unsure and the message is taken less seriously.

Minimisers are words like 'just', 'only', 'a bit' and 'a little'. Overuse of these words, especially when talking about yourself, can play down what you are saying, especially in the context of achievements, results or experience. Underplaying results, for example, can either undermine your credibility or sound like false modesty, which can be as damaging as overplaying your achievements and coming across as bragging.

Like

The interesting thing about language is that it is constantly changing and evolving.

Millennial women have often been criticised for using language in a professional sphere that older generations perceive as making them sound unprofessional. Frequent use of the word 'like' is a classic example. It is used for so much more than the dictionary definition of 'akin to or similar to something'. Sometimes it is used as a filler, similar to making 'hmm' or 'er' sounds to allow your voice to catch up with your mind and give you breathing space to process how to articulate a certain thought.

It is also used in many other ways:

- 'I was so, like, amazed.'

- 'That's, like, such a bad thing...'

- 'And she was, like, "I don't really know and I was like", well you should know.'

One millennial journalist described a conversation with another older male journalist who said to her: 'If you say "like" one more time I'm going to lose my rag!' She reported feeling ridiculed and undermined by the encounter. The actress Emma Thompson has been vocal about 'sloppy' use of language, as she believes the overuse of 'like' to be.

There has, however, been much debate over whether women use this more than men and whether some people's dislike of this way of using the language is fair or legitimate. Is it just another excuse to 'police' women's speech or silence it? The evidence from several linguists, Deborah Cameron for example, is that women do not use contemporary types of expression more than their male counterparts.

Many commentators have said that the frequent use of 'like' undermines young women's credibility and makes them sound unprofessional. Constant use can be perceived as irritating and distracting. Given that we know the assumption tends to be that men automatically have professional credibility while women often have to prove and demonstrate theirs, anything that causes an audience to question credibility hurts women more than men.

The wider point here is about the generational relationship to language. The use of colloquial language by a younger generation, whether men or women, in front of older generations in a professional setting is going to cause a clash of styles. Women may well get a harder time for it than men, but the point is simply this: if you want or need to influence older generations who typically find this use of language irritating, then you need to flex your language appropriately, a bit like not swearing in front of your granny or not wearing sequins to a meeting with corporate bankers.

What to do

Avoid self-effacing language

When you are talking about your achievements or experience, own it. Never downplay it. Be willing and able to simply say 'thank you' when you receive any compliment (when you are being introduced as the next speaker, for example).

Avoid self-deprecating language

Avoid the use of 'I'm no expert', 'I'm new to this' or anything else that undermines your professional expertise and credibility. A better approach is to give evidence of your credibility and / or the basis for your comment before sharing your thoughts, eg: 'Based on my knowledge/ expertise...', 'Listening to the group, I'm hearing x, y, z and that leads me to propose / determine / conclude...'

Primacy and recency

The number 1 rule is very simple: NEVER start or finish a speech, presentation or meeting intervention with an apology or self-effacing language. Ideally, use striking and memorable words and images to grab your audience's attention at the beginning and leave them on a high at the end.

Qualifiers and minimisers

A certain amount of fillers, qualifiers or minimisers is not a problem – they are normal and conversational – but watch out and be aware of what you say.

Some of these vocal habits can become noticeable and distracting. You know that moment when you start counting how many times a speaker says a particular word or phrase because it's getting irritating (you have probably done it yourself)? That is when it has become a problem and is distracting from your message and undermining your credibility.

If, having read this, you recognise that you have acquired a tendency to qualify and soften what you say in a professional context, consider consciously choosing strong and definite words instead:

- not 'perhaps', but 'I will'
- 'it is', rather than 'it could be'
- 'I believe it is' rather than 'it may be...'

This is not easy to do. It may take a bit of adjustment. The good news is, however, that being aware of what you tend to tend do will help you self-correct.

'Like' and other slang terms

'Decorum' comes from a Latin word meaning 'the right style for the right occasion'. When thinking about speaking in a meeting or making a speech or presentation, be aware of different styles of language and ask yourself: 'What style is most likely to work well with this audience and deliver the best result for me?' You can develop flexibility to move smoothly between different styles of language, from the formal to the more colloquial, according to your audience, just as you vary how you speak to a child, your boss or your best friend.

Handling 'tone policing'

You need to prepare some thought-through, assertive responses that you call upon when you are challenged and feel 'on the back foot'. Being unprepared often results in defaulting to typical aggressive or passive 'fight-or-flight' limbic responses that are sparked in the moment.

The suggestions below are just that – suggestions. These types of responses need to be authentic for you and put in words and phrases with which you feel comfortable.

- If you simply want to navigate around tone policing, you can simply ignore it and continue making your point as you intended.

- If you want to challenge the tone policing, you can call it out as such and ask why the speaker thinks it is acceptable to tell you how to articulate your views.

- You can name it as tone policing and give the speaker a face saver by saying: 'I don't I think you meant that the way it came out.'

- If, for example, you are called aggressive you could respond with: 'Interesting that you perceive it that way. My perception is that I am merely being direct. But moving on from stylistic differences of opinion...'

CHAPTER 7

Vocal quality

I realise that in commenting on this I risk stepping into a feminist minefield. There are many who would assert that women can and should sound exactly how they want to, and it is not up to anybody else to tell them how they 'should' use their voice. I would have to wholeheartedly agree with that.

It is up to each individual woman to sound how she wishes to. The purpose of this chapter is not to police women or tell them what is 'right' but to make millennial women aware of that amazing instrument they possess (their voice) and how they can use it to best effect in order to achieve their goals.

It is well known that in verbal communication the message we receive when someone speaks does not come solely from the words or language. Studies vary on the precise figures, but the original research suggests that language makes up 7% of the message received, and the voice about 38%.[45]

Whatever the precise percentage, there is widespread agreement that vocal tone is more important for how your message 'lands' than the actual words you say. Vocal quality is therefore an incredibly important topic when it comes to speaking effectively, being heard and being understood.

Volume

> Her voice was ever soft, Gentle and low,
> An excellent thing in a woman.

William Shakespeare, *King Lear*

Volume is not just about audibility. When you are speaking, your volume is as much about presence and authority as it is about audibility. For both men and women finding the right volume for the space you are speaking in is key: too loud and you sound shouty and hectoring; too quiet and you sound timid and uncertain.

I often do an exercise with groups where I get someone to stand at one side of a big room and speak or read something while the rest of the group stands at the opposite end. I ask the speaker at what level of volume they were speaking on a 1-10 scale, 10 being the loudest. I then ask the observers to say what level they perceived it to be. In almost 90% of cases, the speakers think they are much louder than the audience perceive them to be.

Hardly surprising in some ways, given that when we speak, we hear our voices from within our own heads and the audience hears the sound that has travelled through the airwaves. That is also why most people do not think they sound like themselves when they hear a recording or video of themselves. You do experience the sound of your own voice differently from others.

I usually then ask the speaker to try again, this time a level or two louder. What I've found from these exercises and wider observation of listening to hundreds of women speak is that women tend to speak more quietly than men. They find it far more difficult than men to speak at a greater volume in this exercise and often really cannot bring themselves to be significantly louder.

Given the historical context that we have already explored, this is not surprising. Women speaking loudly have been harangued and criticised for sounding strident, shrill, aggressive, or unfeminine. Unfortunately, this continues to be true and, as a result, many continue to speak in quieter tones that command less attention and give them less presence than a voice and volume that can fill a large space. Speaking on digital media, video platforms like

Zoom or You Tube videos also requires enough volume to engage and hold the interest of listeners or viewers.

Pace — speed

Speaking quickly can be a good thing, as it can convey energy and enthusiasm, and make you sound passionate and committed to your topic. Typically, people also speed up when they are nervous, often out of a desire to just get through the presentation — women tend to do it in situations where they feel embattled or unduly anxious.

The downsides of speaking quickly, however, are that your audience can struggle to take in what you are saying and to absorb a stream of information that is coming at them. Good speakers specifically vary their speed to reinforce their message, speaking faster to demonstrate excitement or urgency and slower to suggest something momentous or important.

There have been many claims and assertions but virtually no definitive data on whether men or women speak faster. In fact, gender differences matter a lot less than regional differences — Londoners speaking faster than people from the West Country or New Yorkers speaking faster than folks from North Carolina.

What is the typical words per minute speaking rate? If you google that, you will get a myriad of different answers, but in the UK, the range is between 140 and 180 words per minute. Speaking at rates consistently above 160 to 190 wpm is where is gets harder to absorb content.

Really great speakers are usually slower, at around 100 wpm. Martin Luther King's iconic speech was given at 100 wpm, Churchill's famous speech about fighting on the beaches and landing grounds at 116 wpm. In the 2008 democratic primaries, Hillary Clinton spoke at a rapid pace of 160 wpm that compared unfavourably to Barack Obama's 90 wpm, which made him sound weighty and statesmanlike and her sound edgy and hurried.

The key thing to note for millennial women in professional contexts is that there is a correlation between speed of speech and gravitas. People perceived to have gravitas (ie to be weighty, deserving of respect and of being listened to) are usually slower speakers. Their pace of speech signals that they are confident, in control and not to be hurried or rushed. Given women need to work harder to prove credibility, a slower pattern of speech can be helpful.

Modulation

Modulation is the variation we put into our vocal tone. A varied vocal tone (in terms of pitch, pace, volume and rhythm) is one you will find engaging. You will be more willing and able to listen to the speaker and more likely to look favourably on what they have to say.

The opposite of a well-modulated tone is a monotone. I'm sure everyone has had the misfortune of having to listen to someone who speaks in a flat tone that is the auditory equivalent of Valium. It sends you into that kind of meeting or conference coma in which minutes or hours can pass and you have no recollection of what was said during that time.

Most people naturally speak with a good degree of modulation in their voice. In workshops I ask people to read from children's books (*The Gruffalo* being my favourite) because almost everyone really gets into it, has fun and uses some silly voices. They prove to themselves that they do indeed have the capability to use good vocal variation.

What happens, though, is that anxiety and digital media can flatten you out into a monotone, which is unfortunate and creates the opposite effect to what you need. Giving a speech or presentation requires more energy, 'drama' and vocal variation in order to come across as engaging – the bigger the audience, the bigger the need for variation and emphasis in how you speak.

The excellent voice coach who works with me once had a conversation with a client who felt awkward because she was rehearsing for a presentation to a large audience and we were encouraging her to increase her level of modulation. That felt strange and unnatural to her compared to her normal conversational style. To reassure her the voice coach said: 'You won't sound weird, you'll just sound interesting.'

I always use the metaphor of stage makeup. When you see it up close it looks awful, overdone and even comical, but it works perfectly at a distance so you can see facial expressions on stage. Similarly, your vocal tone has to be exaggerated compared to your normal conversational style to work well when speaking to any medium to large group.

Voice and digital media.

The 2020 COVID-19 crisis and resulting global lockdowns have accelerated the widespread adoption of digital meeting and video platforms like Teams, Zoom, Go To Meeting and Skype. Video communication and the use of You Tube, once the preserve of teenagers teaching gaming skills and makeup, are now ubiquitous in the professional world.

Digital media increase the flattening effect on your voice. On these platforms, we have also all effectively become newsreaders, as you can only be seen from the chest upwards (if you want to work in your pyjamas, then this is a good thing!), which means that you lose most of the effect of body language and have to rely more on your voice to convey the full meaning of your words.

You have to work your voice much harder. Take for example the phrase 'this project has the potential to double our business'. It can be interpreted in different ways. Do you mean that the listeners should choose this particular project as opposed to a competing project? In this case, you would vocally stress the word 'this': '**this** project has the potential to double our business'. Or do you mean that it is so big it can't be ignored? 'This project has the potential to **double** our business.'

The emphasis you put on key words is critical to conveying your meaning. The emphasis required on digital media is even greater than in face-to-face interactions. Often women in particular are uncomfortable with what they perceive to be the theatricality of giving this level of punch or emphasis to their words. It can make people feel unnatural and a bit silly.

Uptalk and vocal fry

One area of controversy in recent years has been around the tendency of millennials to use a form of modulation called by some linguists 'uptalk' or what had been called AQI, Australian Questioning Intonation.

Traditionally, in English a flat tone is used for statements, an upward intonation means a question and a downward tone suggests a command. When asking your audience a rhetorical question, your voice would normally rise towards the end of the sentence. To say something directive or make an assertion, you would probably use a downward intonation to sound more assertive and commanding.

Uptalk is the vocal habit of using an upward tone at the end of your sentence more frequently than just when asking a question. This originally came from regional intonations in Australia and California but it has become more of a generational phenomenon thanks to TV and films.

Vocal fry is using the lowest register of your voice by relaxing the vocal cords without increasing the amount of air you are pushing through, which produces slower vibration and a lower, sometimes creaky sound to the voice. What does this sound like? Think Kim Kardashian, Paris Hilton or most of the cast of *Made in Chelsea*.

The use of these intonation styles by millennial women has been the subject of much controversy. Author Naomi Wolf wrote an article in *The Guardian* in which she reflected a popular view of older generations that the use of these vocal styles is undermining the professional credibility of millennial women. She said: 'Vocal fry is that guttural growl at the back of the throat, as a Valley girl might sound if she had been shouting herself hoarse at a rave all night. The less charitable refer to it privately as painfully nasal, and to young women in conversation sounding like ducks quacking. "Vocal fry" has joined more traditional young-women voice mannerisms such as run-ons, breathiness and the dreaded question marks in sentences (known by linguists as uptalk) to undermine these women's authority in newly distinctive ways.'[46]

The issue with uptalk is that it can sound like the speaker is constantly asking questions, lacking confidence in what they are saying and therefore articulating their thoughts as questions rather than statements. To some, it can make the speaker sound like they are insecure and needing constant responses and reassurance in answer to their questions. Users of uptalk would not interpret it as constant questioning, just a way of talking.

The problem with vocal fry is that it can make the speaker come across as finding the conversation unbearably tedious, like a sort of bored insouciance sometimes associated with upper class Englishmen, like the fictional Lord Sebastian Flyte from *Brideshead Revisited* or perhaps MP Jacob Rees-Mogg.

The backlash against Wolf's article was significant, with many, including linguists like Deborah Cameron, saying that women should not be criticised or judged for their vocal style, and doing so was merely another form of silencing women that should be rejected: 'This endless policing of women's language – their voices, their intonation patterns, the words they use, their syntax – is uncomfortably similar to the way our culture polices women's bodily appearance.

Just as the media and the beauty industry continually invent new reasons for women to be self-conscious about their bodies, so magazine articles and radio programmes encourage a similar self-consciousness about our speech.'[47]

There are three key points here:

1. It is true that uptalk and vocal fry are not unique to women, millennial men also adopt this style. It is therefore interesting that most, although not all, criticism of it is targeted at women. It is indicative of what Cameron calls the greater 'policing' of women when they speak and symptomatic of the 4,000-year-old silence project.

2. It is true that this is a generational shift. Language is mutable and so is vocal style, and clashes between the generations in terms of what they like and prefer are inevitable.

3. For millennial women, the issue is that the people currently in senior professional roles around them still belong to the generation that dislikes uptalk and vocal fry. When you make a statement such as 'I think we should invest in this promotional programme', you want that to sound compelling and like you are totally convinced that it is the best course of action. Uptalk is still interpreted by many as a questioning intonation. Sounding like you are questioning your own assertion weakens and undermines your point and risks damaging your authority and preventing people from perceiving you as a leader or credible

authority. Vocal fry is interpreted by many as sounding bored or superior and therefore conveying a lack of interest and commitment, which again dents your ability to persuade and bring people with you.

Pitch

Pitch is another fraught topic for women. Women's voices are of course naturally higher than men's and it is received wisdom that speaking in a lower pitch typically sounds more powerful, so that people (both men and women) associate these tones with leaders and leadership. Speaking in stentorian tones is standard practice for male leaders.

In the cultural context of men holding positions of power and leadership roles for millennia, and women not being in these roles until the last five or six decades, it is unsurprising that this correlation between vocal tone and authority still exists for many.

Women's voices that are high and often get higher still as a reaction to anxiety are often criticised for sounding 'shrill', 'screechy', 'high pitched', 'shrieky' or 'like a harpy'.

The evolution of Margaret Thatcher's voice is a case in point. She clearly understood the correlation between perception of command and lower vocal pitch. In footage from her early career as an MP in the 60s, we hear a quite high-pitched voice and 'feminine' softness of tone. By 1975, as she rose in the Conservative Party, she was using a voice coach to lower the pitch of her voice, sounding, to many at the time, more authoritative and commanding. In the words of one voice expert: 'We hear the steely quality of those more strident bright tones lending her greater command. The voice has a winning vocal recipe of strength, calmness and determination.'

By the time she was Prime Minister in the early 80s her voice was lower still. It is said that she did not do as much of the after-dinner speaking circuit as other former leaders because she had damaged her voice from all those years of forcing it into a lower register than was natural for her.

Hillary Clinton was frequently accused of having an annoying voice in the 2016 presidential election. There was little or no comment on the quality of Donald Trump's vocal tone.

Much of this criticism of pitch is wholly unfair and merely symptomatic of the world not having had enough female leaders to change people's perceptions. There is some evidence to suggest that the negative perception of women's voices is not in fact due to their actual voices but often due to technology.

In *Invisible Women*, Caroline Criado-Perez makes the case that men are the default consideration for design and women the exception.[48] In the same way, Professor Tom McEnaney, from University of California at Berkley, says the US has a long history of men criticising the way women speak. According to him, sound technologies, starting with the gramophone and phonograph all the way up to today's digital audio technologies, are developed and optimised for men's voices. So unsurprisingly, listeners perceive men's voices as more attractive than women's.[49]

What to do

Volume – speak louder!

Get an understanding of your normal range, get some input to help you calibrate your default volume and, if you speak quietly, work on developing the capacity for more volume. Increased volume requires breathing deeply (diaphragmatic breathing as opposed to breathing higher up in your chest) to get enough oxygen in the tank to be able to produce more volume. It is also about moving your lips well, opening your mouth widely to enunciate the words clearly. You should not be forcing your vocal cords.

Speed

Consider your pace. How many words per minute do you typically speak at? If you do not know, time yourself or use a software that will give you some analysis of how fast you speak. Ask for feedback. If you do tend to speak quite quickly and want to convey more gravitas, then look to slow your pace of speech.

I never advocate that you try to fundamentally alter a core part of your speaking style. That would be asking you to bend yourself out of shape and if you do that, the result is usually not an authentic sound (as well as being hard to maintain). You can. however. make some adjustment when it matters or when you have a particular message to convey at a certain event.

If you like to speak quickly and that is your 'default' style, one way of slowing your perceived rate of speech is to pick one or more passages for which you want to consciously slow down. Adding some pauses also allows your audience to catch up and will slow the overall perception of the speed of speech. A few slower passages and more pauses will allow a fast speaker to create enough variation so as to not be thought of as a hurried speaker.

Modulation

Read children's books – one good way to practise and develop your ability to use varied vocal modulation is to read children's books. You can practise with your kids, nieces or nephews, and really go to town when you read to them. Use different voices for different characters, go loud and really quiet. Have some fun. Using a 'Gruffalo'-style voice for a business presentation or political speech is clearly not going to work well, but if you have trained your voice to use more of its capacity, you'll be more comfortable using that wider range.

Plan your modulation – if you're working on an important speech or presentation I'd advise you to write out a full script, use that for initial read throughs, and then condense it into bullet points, using the note section of PowerPoint or index cards for the actual delivery.

If you have written out a full script, then it is also useful to plan your modulation. It can help to write key words in bold, reminding you to give them full emphasis. You might annotate sections to indicate when to go faster to indicate urgency, or slower… to… indicate… seriousness. You can insert symbols (///) to remind you where to pause if you want the audience to fully absorb a key point and to slow the overall pace of your speech.

Uptalk and vocal fry

Your choice here is whether to challenge or navigate. Do you proudly keep hold of the way you choose to talk and challenge those who criticise it? Or do you adapt and navigate the current situation in your workplace?

I would suggest that developing style flexibility as advocated in Chapter 6 for language is equally relevant to vocal style, and developing that will enable you to navigate your environment successfully.

Making pragmatic adaptations does not mean surrendering to the patriarchy! People adapt to things in professional contexts all the time. A successful salesperson soon learns not to wear a pin-striped power suit when going to a software company or designer jeans and an open-neck shirt to a merchant bank!

You do not talk the same way to a child and a professor. We are perfectly capable of making automatic adaptations, we just need to be able to do that consciously in the workplace.

In order to adapt you will need to develop awareness of your current style. Ensure you record and listen to yourself speaking and note how often your sentences rise at the end or fall into the vocal fry register. Get feedback from colleagues and peers. You should not try to bend yourself out of shape all the time, but simply focus on using these styles less when giving key presentations to mixed or older audiences.

Pitch

It is important that you do not try to force your voice into registers that are not natural or comfortable for you, and neither should you have to. The suggested action here is just to ensure that your voice does not get higher than normal when you are nervous.

Exercises to rid your body of tension (tensing and relaxing your jaw and shoulders, for example) and warming up your voice using tepid, not cold, drinking water can all help. Basic voice exercises like yawning, doing some tongue twisters or singing out loud are all good ways to get your voice ready, perhaps in the privacy of your car en route to the venue.

When using digital media, eg when you are about to join a video conference, try this method shared with me by BBC news presenter Martine Croxall to make the first words you say hit the right pitch: say 'hello my name is…' three times. The first time, say it as high as you can; the second, as low as you can; and the third time, in the middle – that will be your most natural tone and the one you want to start off with. That small exercise will stop you making a squeaky start to a call – you do not want the first time you use your voice in a day to be the time it matters.

The other key thing to work on, particularly on digital media, is diction. When you are giving a presentation on a digital platform such as Zoom, people cannot see much of you. Typically, your audience will see your slide and your head will be in a tiny video box in the top right-hand corner. This means that virtually all of your message must come across from your voice and words. Articulating clearly involves moving your mouth and lips more than you usually do.

With all of these vocal elements, the tactics outlined here will be useful to you. If you feel you really want or need to work on your vocal skills, I thoroughly recommend working with a voice coach early in your career. They can be an excellent investment to ensure you establish vocal habits that are helpful and congruent to your style, and will also keep your voice in good shape, especially if speaking is an important part of your career.

CHAPTER 8

Body language

In Chapter 7 we saw how, in verbal communication, the voice is responsible for about 40% of the message the listener receives. Body language is usually acknowledged to account for somewhere around 50% of the message.

Body language is a hugely broad topic. It can encompass clothing, eye contact, posture, hand and arm gestures, stance, movement, positioning – the list is extensive.

Why is body language so important? My mum always told me that first impressions count, and it turns out that in light of contemporary neuroscience, she was absolutely right.

Why this is so dates back to our primeval ancestors. Early humans had to decide instantly whether something in front of them (a sabre-toothed tiger, a tyrannosaurus rex, a rival tribe) was a threat to survival. Making that instant judgment enabled humans to immediately make fight, flight or freeze responses that were critical to survival.

These judgments came from the limbic system, the automatic response part of the brain that is driven by what is felt, not conscious thought. These innate human reactions are still there. We still instantly evaluate people and decide whether we like them (which equates to whether we perceive them not to be a threat to us) or not (we think they are a threat).

There was a story told on this instant judgment reflex. A new class of students were asked to assess their lecturer, after he had delivered the first minute of his lecture. The lecture and the rest of the term continued. At the end of the whole term, when the students were again asked to evaluate the lecturer, their views had hardly changed at all.

The bald truth is that we make instant judgments based on what we see. When you stand up to speak, especially in a situation where you're speaking to strangers in a meeting or presentation environment, people are going to make judgments about you. This can feel quite unsettling, particularly in light of what we discussed in Chapter 5 about how women are judged much more harshly and personally. The criticism is often simply about the way you look. It is yet another contributory factor to why so many women do not like to speak up in public or feel so self-conscious when they do.

Another, more positive aspect of body language is that people read and internalise the messages of body language at a subconscious level. Body language that emits confidence and status is a good way for women to project power and authority in a subtle, unspoken way. If you can do this, then you can enhance your perceived credibility and authority without having to use forceful language or tone (and without exposing yourself to potential criticism).

Mastering body language is an important aspect of being able to speak in public and ensuring you are being heard.

Space – stance and staging

A basic rule of gender stereotypes is that big in a man = good, big in a woman = bad. The typical stereotype of feminine and attractive is a petite, lean woman. A tall, solid, powerful man also ticks all the boxes of the positive male stereotype.

As a result, women tend to take up less space. If you need proof of this, I won't offer data, I'll invite you to take a trip on a crowded bus or tube train. You'll see women sitting with knees clasped tightly together, hands folded in their lap to take up the minimum space. You'll see men 'manspsreading', ie with their legs spread wide, not caring how much space they take up; in fact it often seems their thinking is the more, the better!

Or check out the line-up on the *Graham Norton Show* or any other talk show sofa. The female guests will be all self-contained, with neatly crossed legs and often sitting forward; the men will be sprawled out, lounging back, arms across the back of the sofa. In the average meeting, men will have their files, iPads, etc scattered across the table, taking up territory. Women are more likely to have neat piles and stay within 'their' space, directly in front of them.

In public speaking, women's stances typically reflect the small = good stereotype. A common stance is standing with one leg crossed over the other at the ankles and one arm holding the other arm, the torso slightly hunched down and the head slightly lowered. These are classic defensive poses in terms of body language. In early human terms, they protect us physically by making us a smaller target and showing due deference to the dominant silver-backed gorilla, who might then feel less inclined to attack!

Women also tend to stand more behind lecterns and move less around the available space on stage. All of these defensive aspects of body language reflect nerves and anxiety felt by both men and women when speaking, but which tend to be amplified in women because a) women often feel greater anxiety as a result of the need to be perfect and the greater likelihood of criticism and b) they help women subconsciously conform to the 'small' stereotype.

Men and women can all display nerves by fiddling with things. Men typically tend to play with change in their pockets, for example. Women can display nerves by fiddling with or flicking their hair, which can be interpreted as very girlish or even flirtatious and can therefore detract from the impression of a professional woman who has seriousness and gravitas.

Nervous body language is less apparent in online meetings and presentations, given we can't see most of the body. However, fiddling with your hair and waving your hands about are very apparent and distracting, and therefore to be avoided.

Such defensive body language undermines your credibility as a speaker.

They convey your anxiety to your audience – think back to a time when you have watched a nervous speaker. How did you feel? It is not a comfortable feeling watching someone suffering from acute nervousness. No audience likes it, it does not make them feel secure, in fact it makes them feel uncomfortable or nervous on the speaker's behalf. It gets in the way of people listening to the message.

Nervous body language does not make you look like a leader, an expert or someone to be listened to – there is a big correlation between confidence and competence. Tomas Chamorro-Premuzic, Professor of Business Psychology at Columbia University and UCL, says that people tend to equate leadership and competence with confidence.

Most men (raised in the prince paradigm to be brave and fearless) tend to be better at portraying confidence, even when they do not feel it. They are not socialised to be as self-critical as women and so often do feel nervous but mask it with a display of more outward confidence. In fact, this masking leads many men to appear to have more confidence than actual competence.

That is a central theme of Tomas's book *Why Do So Many Incompetent Men Become Leaders?* He says: 'People tend to equate leadership with the very behaviours, overconfidence for example, that often signal bad leadership. What is more, these behaviours are more common in the average man than the average woman'.[50]

Nervous and constrained body language becomes self-fulfilling. You feel anxious, so you cross your legs, which makes your body feel unbalanced, wobbly, not safe on your own legs. You then hug one arm with the other, making you feel tight, your lungs and your breathing feel restricted, which makes you feel bad and therefore more anxious.

Gestures

Part of the small = good paradigm also relates to arm and hand gestures. You can think of the range of arm movements falling into three zones: zone 1 is hands above the head; zone 2, arms between head and waist; and zone 3, arms below the waist.

Women tend to make smaller gestures than men, with most female gestures staying in zone 2. This is sometimes exacerbated by women keeping their elbows tucked tightly into their sides or their hands clasped together in another classic defensive pose. Occasionally using bigger gestures, being more visually expansive and getting into zone 1 or 3 is a good way to project more confidence and authority.

Face and eyes

Eyes

The eyes are the window to the soul. They are important in any communication, and particularly in presentations. Making eye contact with your audience engages them, commands their attention and makes them feel like you are talking to them.

The issue here is that some women feel that direct eye contact is challenging or confrontational in some way. The traditional demure woman of old had her eyes cast down and looked up tentatively from under her fringe – think Lady Diana in the early 1980s! The press at the time lapped it up – 'shy-Di', perfect, demure princess material. This has not yet gone away: the 2018 EY women's development programme I referenced earlier gave advice that 'If you're having a conversation with a man, don't talk to a man face-to-face. Men see that as threatening.'

Another reason both men and women avoid eye contact is simply that direct eye contact makes the audience very real and present to you, and there is nowhere to hide. This can increase people's anxiety levels. Many people rapidly scan the audience or deploy that distant look known as the '1,000-yard stare'. Scanning and letting your eyes dart about the audience can actually cause an overload of visual stimulus and increase anxiety.

On the other hand, looking directly at your audience and engaging individuals in direct eye contact, slowly and steadily, are critical for holding your audience's attention and conveying your authority. Making eye contact when speaking in a meeting is similarly important.

Smiling

Smiling is often a good thing. If you're smiling during a presentation, it usually conveys positive emotions. It says you are confident and glad to be there. Positivity and confidence are infectious and tend to rub off on the audience, making them feel relaxed, happy and more inclined to buy into what you have to say. Smiling can also cause you to feel happier and relaxed.

Smiling is what women do well. Another lesson from the princess paradigm is that part of being a perfect woman involves smiling – a lot! The traditional people-pleasing ideal of womanhood that is kind, nurturing, gentle and soft is always a joy to be around and smiles constantly. The person who told Huff Post about the EY training course mentioned above said that 'It felt like we were being turned into someone who is "super-smiley", who never confronts anyone.'

However, 'oversmiling' can undermine your effectiveness. It many circumstances, even when women have something serious, challenging, controversial or difficult to say, many may still feel the need to smile. You may be doing it on purpose to soften a hard message, or perhaps subconsciously to avoid coming across as too harsh or forceful and avoid the critical 'unfeminine' label, but this can weaken the strength of your message and, in serious circumstances, gravitas and smiling rarely go together.

At the height of the COVID-19 pandemic in the UK there was an interview on *Good Morning Britain* on ITV between Piers Morgan and the government minister responsible for the care sector, Helen Whatley. The interview took place via Zoom. Piers Morgan held up a newspaper with a dramatic headline about deaths in care homes. Helen Whatley could not see it as she was speaking directly to the camera on her laptop. He berated her and said the government was callous and uncaring about the plight of old people in care homes. She tried to explain that she could not see what he was showing but he did not let her speak – and she smiled. Morgan went for her, suggesting she found the situation funny. Why did she smile? Clearly, she was not smiling at the awful and tragic situations of old people dying, suggesting that was absurd, a 'shock-jock style' rating booster.

She did not smile because she was enjoying Morgan's bully-boy, berating tactics. She smiled, perhaps, because women are supposed to. Perhaps, as an experienced politician, she knew that she would only be criticised if she angrily bit back at him, so instead she took it and smiled.

To not smile is to contravene the stereotype of a successful woman. Women who look serious, or who are concentrating intensely, are often criticised for looking angry or unpleasant. Something that has been captured in that peculiarly unpleasant, gendered phrase 'resting bitch face'. There is no male equivalent for this.

In her book *Becoming*, Michelle Obama talks about a time during her husband's first presidential campaign when, despite attracting huge, enthusiastic audiences to hear her speak everywhere she went, she had been getting some negative feedback from the media on her speaking style.

She describes how one of her husband's advisors pulled her into a meeting and had her watch a video of her speech with the sound off. 'I saw myself speaking with intensity and conviction and never letting up. I always addressed the tough times many Americans were facing. My face reflected the seriousness of what I believed was at stake, but it was too serious, too severe, *at least given what people were conditioned to expect from a woman.*'[51]

She articulates what many women face, particularly in politics and senior management – another double bind. They are condemned if don't look smiley and happy, a stern-looking woman risks all kinds of unwelcome epithets such as ice maiden, cold or frigid, yet women are also condemned as lightweight and fluffy when they do smile.

Clothing

Clothing and appearance are huge topics for women. Men merely wear the standard suit, tie and smart shirt uniform and nobody comments on their appearance. Hillary Clinton calculated that in order to conform to what was expected of a woman's appearance in the public eye, she was obliged to spend the equivalent of 25 days on hair, clothes and makeup over the 18-month 2016 presidential election campaign!

I am not going to comment on what your wardrobe should be, that is far too much of an individual choice to be able to comment on helpfully. You do, however, need to give some consideration to what you wear for speeches with microphones, for speeches or presentations with a raised stage, and for online presentations.

If you are giving a big speech or presentation in a venue that requires microphones, especially microphones that you wear instead of hold, you need to remember that those, like so much else in the world, are designed for men. They work on the assumption that you will be wearing something with a strong waistband or pocket that will house the microphone battery pack and a jacket with a lapel to which to fix the actual microphone – typically a bit of an issue if you are wearing a dress or a lightweight fabric blouse.

I have worked with women who have ingeniously managed to improvise by hooking it to the top of their tights or the back of their dress if they have long hair to cover it. Wherever they have found to house the pack has never been ideal! So, if you're speaking at that type of event, you might want to wear a skirt with a robust waistband and jacket. Consider the choice of tops, select a blouse that isn't sheer silk and going to be destroyed by (or struggle to support) the pinned-on microphone, and avoid polo necks that don't really have anywhere to support a microphone.

Wearing a skirt or dress when you are on a stage and the audience is seated below you could give the front few rows the perfect opportunity for upskirting! Again, consider your wardrobe choices or be very careful where you move, and don't get too close to the front of the stage.

In online meetings and presentations, at least all you've got to worry about is your top. Just beware of clothes with a strong geometric pattern (stripes, lines, dog-tooth check), which can cause a visual blurring and wobbly effect on digital media. It can be quite hypnotic, and not in a good way! Ideally, you want to wear something relatively plain, so as not to distract attention from you and what you're saying.

Also think about your background for a digital meeting or presentation. A white blouse against a backdrop of magnolia walls is likely to make you disappear or look like a ghostly, disembodied head. If you're blonde as well, it's even worse! Think about something that will contrast with your background.

What to do

Space, stance and staging

Conventional wisdom says that your physiology (your body) follows your psychology (your thoughts), eg you feel nervous and therefore you display defensive body language.

The mind-body connection is complex. Proponents of NLP (neuro-linguistic programming) say that you can reverse this, your body can drive your mind and adopting confident body language will affect how you think and feel. If you are hunched up, change your body position to a more fully upright stance and throw your shoulders back and it will start making you feel better, more positive and more confident. Try it and see!

I am not advocating that women take up the 'power stance' with hands on hips, legs planted wide apart and groin thrust forward. For females, it is perhaps only Wonder Woman who can really rock that look! Even for men it has become a bit of a cliché.

However, a balanced stance is worth adopting. This means ensuring that when you speak, your weight is balanced across both legs, hip width apart, so that you do not sway or wobble.

This type of balanced stance has a positive psychological effect as well: it makes you feel grounded and, on a psychological level, stable and safe, which in turn makes you feel less anxious and more confident.

It is worth mentioning shoes as well. High heels do not help you feel balanced and grounded when speaking. Heels make some women feel good about themselves, but when it comes to breathing, alignment and balance they are not a good thing.

Shoes can be an emotional issue. If you are a woman who hyperventilates at the thought of having to wear flatties for presentations, this may be an issue. Voice coach Sally Bishop said she once worked with a woman who teared up at the suggestion that she might have to take off her stilettos, and that was only in practice! We could, perhaps, compromise by suggesting you wear wedges or the lowest heels in your wardrobe.

Many meetings are conducted sitting down, but in the bigger meetings, panels or Q&A-type sessions, consider standing up to make your point. It will give you presence and make you look commanding, and it helps with voice projection.

Movement

Come out from behind the lectern and make use of the available space when you speak.

The reasons people stay rooted in one place are both psychological and logistical. Psychologically, it's the fear of being seen and taking up space. Hiding behind the lectern or the table can feel safer and less exposed than striding out to centre stage, but guess what? People are still looking at you, they can still see you and being static does not add to the variety, energy and impact of your presentation or speech.

Equally, you don't want to go to the other extreme and start pacing the stage like a caged animal. How much you move needs to be authentic and in keeping with your style. The extrovert will probably be comfortable moving more than the introvert, for example.

Think about movement as part of your planning. If you don't already know where you'll be speaking, try to find out as much as possible about the space. If you can, get into the space, room, stage, etc before you have to deliver a big speech or presentation. Walk round the room, seeing it from different angles. Notice what you can see of the stage or lectern from the back.

Make note of the space you have to work with and what constraints you may have to work around, eg fixed microphones or lack of space at the front of the room where you'll present from. That will enable you to determine how much movement is possible or desirable. This kind of familiarisation also helps make you feel grounded and comfortable in the space.

One good use of movement is moving to a different spot on the stage at the same time you come to a new, key point. That way you create a visual reinforcement of the structure of your presentation. You might move more when you're speaking about the urgency of a situation, for example, or remain static when you're making the key point you want people to remember.

Do not leave movement to chance, think it through as part of your preparation.

Face – smiling

This is a classic 'challenge or navigate' situation – when you speak with intensity, look serious and don't smile, you know you risk being judged as less likeable and more of an ice queen. It should not be the case, but as Michelle Obama found out, it still is.

You may feel that this is unfair and want to challenge this. One approach is to use the refutation technique mentioned in Chapter 5, which could sound something like: 'Today, I want to address a very serious issue. It's not light, it's not fun, in fact, it is tragic. And I make no apology for not playing the traditional role of a happy, smiling woman today.' Or you could say: 'You'll forgive me if today my tone and demeanour are solemn and unsmiling, because…'

The 'navigate' approach would be to ensure that your speech, presentation or meeting comments contain a blend of serious and heavy, and light and bright. This is effectively what Michelle Obama did, with much success. 'Stephanie counselled me to play to my strengths and to remember what I most enjoyed talking about, which was my love for my husband and kids, my connection with working mothers and my proud Chicago roots.'

Your choice of whether to challenge or navigate will be driven by your circumstances, the context and your objectives. Being aware of the double-edged sword of smiling when speaking will enable you to make a thoughtful, conscious choice.

As much as most people don't like watching clips of themselves, getting video of yourself giving your speeches, presentations (and even your questions and meeting responses) is invaluable for enabling you to see yourself as others do and determining if there are any tweaks you want to make to enhance your effectiveness.

Online meetings usually have a recording feature, so that is relatively easy. In live situations, enlist a friend or colleague to film you. You might even want to watch the video back without sound, like Michelle Obama did. It will enable you to observe and be aware of not only your facial expressions, but also any tics or habits you have but may not be aware of that could prove distracting to your listeners.

CHAPTER 9

Emotion and empathy

Men are governed by lines of intellect,
women by curves of emotion.

James Joyce

Joyce was paraphrasing from Oscar Wilde's play *An Ideal Husband* 1895 in expressing a common perception that men are logical and women are emotional. Is this true?

Daniel Goleman, who wrote the seminal book *Emotional Intelligence* in 1996, said in more recent times: 'There are many tests of emotional intelligence, and most seem to show that women tend to have an edge over men when it comes to these basic skills for a happy and successful life.'[52]

However, he and other more up-to-date researchers suggest there is nothing fundamentally different about men's and women's brains or physiology. It is not so much that men and women experience more or less emotion, it is more a case of men and women being socialised to behave and respond differently to the emotions they feel.

As we've seen in previous chapters, women are socialised to be the ones who must show gentleness, concern for others, compassion and kindness. Women have historically had to be people pleasers. It is therefore unsurprising that women tend to be more attuned to the emotions of others. They recognise them and they look to accommodate or assuage, show empathy and make others feel better.

Men are socialised to be brave (back to the prince principle), to hide their emotions for fear of seeming weak. Men do feel emotion but have been trained from birth to put emotions aside and focus on practical solutions. 'Man up', 'grow a pair', etc are phrases that capture these societal expectations.

It is true to say that narrow gender stereotypes hurt both men and women. Things are clearly changing and millennial men in many developed countries tend to feel much freer to express emotion, but cultural and societal norms are so ingrained they are still pervasive and still dominate behaviours and thinking.

Displaying emotion

If men's and women's brains are not fundamentally different, James Joyce is therefore well out of order. And yet, that quote still reflects many of the underlying social norms and beliefs that women are essentially emotional creatures. It is another stick used to beat women with and silence them. It enables men and some other women to dismiss what a woman has to say without actually having to engage in the logic or the argument itself – you can simply dismiss what a woman has said by invalidating the speaker by labelling her as emotional.

It is so much harder for women to be heard when they have to contend with being described in such dismissive terms as 'hysterical', 'moody', 'hormonal', 'drama queen', 'temperamental' or 'irrational'.

A classic demonstration of this was the use of the phrase 'calm down, dear'. This was popularised in a series of commercials for car insurance in 2011 when critic and director Michael Winner was shown leering at young women while driving, consequently colliding with another car and then dealing with the outraged female car driver by saying, 'Calm down, dear, it's only a commercial.' It was intended to be humorous, but in fact it was reflecting and amplifying the stereotype that the woman (whose car had just been hit) was behaving in a hysterical and unacceptable way and therefore Winner was perfectly justified in telling her to be less emotional!

It was one thing for a louche, older director to use the phrase in a commercial that was partly poking fun at him, but it got worse. Later in 2011, the then UK Prime Minister David Cameron, who at the time was in his early 40s, told a female Labour MP, Angela Eagle, to 'calm down, dear' in Parliament.

Cameron was supposed to represent the 'new man' generation but still clearly thought this was a perfectly acceptable way to negate the point a woman was making. When challenged over the innate sexism of his comment, far from apologising he doubled down, saying: 'I will not apologise, she does need to calm down.' Subsequently, a Number 10 spokesman told reporters: 'It was a humorous remark.' This encapsulates the way in which the emotional woman stereotype is still present and used to silence or negate female voices.

'Hard' emotions

Here's the rule: women are free to express 'authorised', soft emotions (gentleness, kindness, etc) but they are not allowed to express 'hard' emotions such as anger or frustration. When a woman articulates anger while speaking in public, it is frowned upon and criticised or derided.

Serena Williams felt the full force of this when she made angry remarks during a game at the US Open tennis tournament. Male players, from John McEnroe onwards, have frequently got angry on court and occasionally received warnings, but few, if any, have faced the barrage of media criticism and $17,000 fine that Serena Williams did.

Recent research has provided data to support what most women already knew: 'Our results lend scientific support to a frequent claim voiced by women, sometimes dismissed as paranoia: that people would have listened to her impassioned argument, had she been a man. The Hillary's sic (Clinton) of the world may feel the need to keep stifling their anger when people ask annoying questions, while the Donald's sic (Trump) can let their rants go unchecked. And the ordinary woman who wishes to be heard may have to suppress her passion, no matter how strongly she feels about her point of view.'[53]

Michelle Obama's passionate speeches in favour of her husband's presidential campaigns caused her to be classified as 'angry', that socially unacceptable emotion for women, and especially women of colour. She captured the challenges of intersectionality. 'I was female, black and strong which translated only to angry, it was another damaging cliché… an unconscious signal not to listen to what we've got to say.'

It can be hard to be heard as a woman, but twice as hard if you are a woman of colour, as you are potentially in receipt of both gender and racial biases. In her book *Becoming*, Michelle Obama went on to capture brilliantly how self-fulfilling this double bind becomes: 'How many "angry black women" have been caught in the circular logic of that phrase. When you aren't being listened to, why wouldn't you get louder. If you're written off as angry and emotional, doesn't that cause more of the same?'[54]

This is the hard truth. As a woman, if you believe in something passionately, whether it's a political point of view or a business strategy, and you want to speak passionately, if you're outraged at some injustice, if you want to be heard and not dismissed, you still have to self-edit and be cautious over how you articulate those emotions.

However, in another case of double bind, when women are unemotional, they get criticised for that too. Former British Prime Minister Theresa May was criticised for being unemotional and the unflattering media epithet, the 'Maybot', was widely used to disparage her.

Terms like 'cold', 'ice maiden', 'frigid' are used to pigeonhole women who fail to display enough of the 'right' emotion when speaking in public.

Reviewing this landscape, it seems a pretty depressing picture for millennial women, and yet, not all is bleak.

Harnessing emotion

The flip side of this is that because of all the societal norms and conditioning, women are on average better at all of the aspects of emotional intelligence, self-awareness, managing emotions, empathy and social skills. Women are typically more willing to articulate emotion, and this does have advantages that they are able to harness and leverage.

As far back as the ancient Greeks, the power of using emotion to persuade has been recognised. You can make a logical and evidential argument but it will usually not influence as much as emotion. Emotion appeals to the automated reaction part of the brain, the limbic system.

Salespeople work to the old and still incredibly accurate adage: 'People buy on emotion and justify on reason.' What this means is that we have an emotional reaction to something (an idea, a person, a proposal) and if we decide we feel positively towards it (we like it, it makes us feel safe, comfortable, excited or not threatened), we then engage our cortex (the logical, thinking part of the human brain) to find data and logical reasons to support what we feel and want to do about that idea, person or proposal.

The decision-making process in humans starts with how we FEEL about something. We think we're making decisions based on reason, logic and data, but in fact, we're not. The brain connects the feeling to the search for data and reasons very quickly and subconsciously, so we are mostly unaware of the initial emotional reaction.

When buying a new car, for example, you might see and fall in love with it and then your cortex will instantaneously take you to appropriate logical arguments, such as 'Well, my old car costs me a lot, it isn't very fuel efficient, it's not environmentally friendly and is probably close to regular breakdowns, which would be very dangerous for me when driving alone in the city late at night.'

Harnessing emotion is a very powerful tool of persuasion. The Greek philosophers, Aristotle in particular, used to talk about logos, pathos and ethos. These were the pillars of Athenian rhetoric, logos being the words, language and logic used; ethos, the credibility, trustworthiness and ethics of the speaker; and pathos, the emotion. When your speech contains a good balance of all of these elements, you are most likely to be a powerful and persuasive speaker.

In the sterile, professional world it is easy to lose sight of the power of emotion and to construct arguments and rationales that are all logos (logic and data) while omitting the ethos and pathos.

I once worked with a CEO who was involved in trying to create a unitary authority in her local council area. It was a battle. It consumed years of effort and hundreds of thousands of pounds and was ultimately unsuccessful. What she told me afterwards was that they subsequently realised that they had relied too much on the data (which they had believed created an irrefutable case) and had not sought to engage emotions.

Being socialised to be aware of emotions, women are better equipped to consider the emotional aspects of an argument, discussion or pitch and harness its power. Women have perhaps not historically played heavily on this, fearing the 'emotional / hysterical' labels, but they certainly have the ability to do so.

Using the audience's emotions

In public speaking, everyone needs to be a people pleaser – the people being the audience. If we establish a good emotional connection with them, they are more likely to listen to us, our thoughts and ideas.

One of my favourite quotes is from Maya Angelou: 'People will forget what you said, forget what you did, they will never forget how you made them feel.' What that tells us is that we need to be attuned to what the audience is feeling, what it wants to hear and how that relates to what you want to say. That should be the start point for planning any presentation or speech.

Giving even brief thought to this applies to questions and comments in meetings. It's what I call 'audience-centric' rather than 'egocentric' speaking. It then enables you to speak in a way that taps into people's emotions and creates a positive and dynamic pull towards you.

Jacinda Ardern, the Prime Minister of New Zealand, gave a brilliant example of the power of using emotion in the wake of the massacre of 50 Muslim worshippers at mosques in Christchurch in 2019. She was strong and took firm and effective action on banning guns in New Zealand, but she was also completely empathic towards the victims, wearing a headscarf out of respect and physically hugging survivors and families of victims.

She has deployed a mix of strength and emotion, and in so doing, she has modelled a style of leadership that has transcended the double bind of emotion. She has found a way to be perceived as strong but not aggressive, empathic but not weak.

There is a huge amount of literature and discussion about the requirements of leadership in the 21st century, in the age of the digital and AI revolutions.

The requirements of work have changed and are still evolving. In the professional world, it is all about knowledge or white-collar work. The demands of a highly educated, millennial workforce with different expectations from previous generations require different communication and leadership styles.

Discussion of the servant-leader style is commonplace in leadership literature. The nature of work today is fluid, project-based, complex and nuanced. Businesses have matrix structures rather than linear lines of control; they are flexible more than rigid. What that means is that empathy, collaboration, team building and emotional intelligence are much more valuable assets than ever before. Command and control as a management style is rapidly dying out. This should enable professional women to thrive by elevating their ability in, and their socialisation around, emotion.

What to do

Displaying emotion

We want to be able to display strong emotions like passion. They say attitudes are infectious, and you want your audiences to catch your passion and positivity. Passion and conviction can and do carry audiences. So how can women do this? How can they walk the tightrope between what is interpreted as positive passion and commitment versus what may be criticised as emotional?

Balance light and dark

Communicate your passion but seek to add moments of lightness. If everything you say is serious and intense, you're more likely to get criticised and, in fairness, it's harder for the audience to absorb. Finding balance when you need to talk about difficult, challenging or upsetting topics is very difficult. In those circumstances, inserting sections that are 'softer' in tone to break up the intensity can make your speech or presentation more comfortable for the audience and less susceptible to criticism.

Have fun

Positive passion can also be about being fun. People are drawn to people, in particular women, with whom they feel relaxed and comfortable, who put them at ease and make them smile. A bit of appropriate humour, moments of lightness can help create this positive energy. It can also help offset the darker or critical aspects of your passion. A relevant anecdote can be useful for this.

Create a vision

It is perhaps more 'acceptable' for women to be positively than negatively passionate. Conveying passion and conviction can be about being positive and upbeat, about making people feel optimistic and hopeful of better things to come. It's about creating and articulating an attractive vision of a future state that people yearn for.

This is effectively what Michelle Obama did during the presidential campaign. She pivoted away from focus on the heavier topics and instead spoke more about her 'safer' topics: husband, children and working mothers.

Although this should not be the case in an ideal, gender-balanced world, it may be worthwhile for you in a particular context where you need to make some compromises in order for your message to be heard and accepted. It worked for Michelle Obama. Yes, she made compromises during the campaign, but she was ultimately successful and is now in an unassailably powerful position, where she can pack auditoriums like the O2 with people who want to hear her speak, and now she can say whatever she likes, however she wants to.

In the challenge versus navigate debate, sometimes you need to lose the battle to win the war. Many of the women I interviewed navigated effectively earlier in their careers, gained success and position, and are now able to challenge more, having achieved positions of power and authority.

Balance

It's important here to balance emotion and logic. Emotion without logic will be perceived as fluffy, superfluous, and lacking in credibility and will attract criticism from men. Logic without emotion is clinical, cold and not something that inspires and captivates. A skilful blend of the two should enable you to harness the power of emotion without the criticism of being emotional.

- Be clear, direct, even forceful when you need to be, but look to balance that with displaying enough empathy and emotion.

- Remember the importance of primacy and recency (what you say first and last having the most impact). To avoid being called emotional, you might start and end with logic, data or facts and make the emotional appeal in the middle. That way, you will have engaged your audience's emotions, but they will be left with the impression that you have been highly logical in your message.

Stealth emotion 1 – using storytelling

Storytelling is an incredibly powerful way to communicate emotion. Stories or narratives have been shared in every culture and in every country throughout history as a means of entertainment, education, preservation of culture and conveying of moral values. Everyone loves a story!

From cave pictures used to communicate a story to ancient Norse tales and modern soap operas, people get involved in a story, they want to know how it ends! Humans have a profound need to tell and hear stories. It is how we share experience, understand each other and create community. If you can illustrate your point(s) using stories, you can convey strong emotions almost subliminally. It allows you to sneak in emotions under the radar!

Third party stories

You can use other people's stories to communicate emotion in a very powerful but third party way; it is harder to criticise you for somebody else's stories.

Fictional stories

These are similar to third party stories; they can be simply made up to illustrate a point. There is something about the way we relax and listen to stories, as we did as children, that makes us accept messages in this format perhaps more readily than information conveyed in factual prose.

Using personal stories

If you tell a story about yourself, your personal experience makes it real. Audiences typically find that engaging. You then come across as a real live person and as such are far more interesting than when speaking as a one-dimensional role or title.

In the midst of the 2020 coronavirus lockdown, the Queen made a speech to the nation from Windsor Castle. She used her personal experience and storytelling as a powerful way to communicate.

The Queen recalled her address to children who were evacuated during the war, when she and her sister were just children themselves. This had an elegant symmetry to it as that broadcast also came from Windsor. She used this very distinct piece of her own personal experience to reinforce the crucial messages about the need for people to stay home and self-isolate to reduce the spread of the virus. She said: 'Today, once again, many will feel a painful sense of separation from their loved ones. But now, as then, we know, deep down, that it is the right thing to do.' She avoided any of the 'who are you to tell us what to do' criticism while powerfully communicating the message of required social distancing.

Stealth emotion 2 – using metaphor

Like stories, metaphors enable you to communicate emotions without being obvious, often without your audience even noticing, as they speak to the unconscious mind. War metaphors, for example: 'the battle before us…', 'we will win this fight with the competition', 'this price war will not defeat us', are frequently used to convey or invoke strong emotions. They are an implicit call to arms to support the speaker. Other metaphors used to convey emotion could, for example, be religious (disciples, messiah, crusade) or fire-related (burning issue, spark of an idea, fanning the flames).

Challenge biased remarks around women and emotion

A theme throughout this book has been to offer you the choice between challenging the current norms and paradigms or simply doing things the way you want to (regardless of the backlash) and seeking to stay congruent and authentic while navigating the issues.

If you are in receipt of criticisms for your communication style or are feeling dismissed or like your ideas and comments are being brushed aside by unjustified emotion labelling, then go ahead and challenge!

- Challenge the relevance:

    o 'I don't see how that has any bearing on the discussion.'

- Calling out unconscious bias:

    o 'I'm sure I must have misheard you, for a moment there I thought you were playing that old "women are too emotional" card!'

- o 'Not that old "women are too emotional" chestnut!'

- o 'I am passionate, she is emotional, they are hysterical!'

- Refocus the discussion:

  - o 'Judgments on emotional state aside, what do we think about the proposal?'

  - o 'I think my emotions are not the point, what is far more important is …'

- Reframing the situation:

  - o 'You call me angry / emotional / temperamental, but what I actually am is passionate, concerned and energetic!'

You should also consider challenging when you hear other women talked about in these terms. If it's about fixing the system (not the just the women), then you should also challenge on behalf of others. In fact, if a group of you are challenging within an organisation, there is safety in numbers and you are more likely to manage to create change.

If, for example, somebody in a meeting or Q&A session says: 'We can't talk about it anymore, she's getting too emotional,' you could reply something like:

- 'I like her passion and think we should continue.'

- 'Nothing wrong with impassioned debate, look at the House of Commons, let's carry on.'

- 'She doesn't seem to be emotional to me, let's get this resolved.'

CHAPTER 10

Behavioural styles

In this book I have outlined the challenges millennial women face when it comes to speaking and being heard. It may be that you will find some areas of this book speak to you very clearly and others less so. There's a reason for that and it has to do with your personality and behavioural style.

Looking at all of these areas in the context of behavioural styles will help you reflect on which of these factors are more or less likely to affect you. Understanding this can help you consciously develop your own speaking style and proactively shape it into a style that is authentically you, that is congruent with your personality and aspirations.

Throughout history humankind has been fascinated by personality.

A brief history of personality profiling tools shows us that that Plato, in 340 BC, had categorised people into four broad types: artisan, guardian, idealist and rational. Galen, in 190 AD, thought the Four Temperaments were: sanguine, melancholic, choleric and phlegmatic. In the mid-16th century, Paracleus in 1550 thought the four areas were: salamanders, gnomes, nymphs and sylphs. This continued with new variations on theme from a wide range of philosophers, thinkers, and psychiatrists including Adickes, Spranger, Kretschmer, Fromm, Freud, Jung, Myers and Briggs, and Marston.[55]

Interestingly, it seems that despite the fact these thinkers come from a variety of cultural contexts, countries and eras, there are actually some consistent threads which seems to reflect that there are some basic and enduring patterns of human personality and behaviour.

My personal preference for looking at behavioural style is to use the DiSC® system as I like its simplicity and ease of use. Like virtually all of these personality and behaviour models (MBTI®, Insights Discovery®, LIFO®), DiSC® is based on a four-box model and shows the interplay between the factors expressed on a sliding scale.

You can be high in any of these traits, but the extent varies. One of the ways in which your DiSC® scores are displayed is in a graph that shows whether you are high in any particular trait – you could be very high in it or just marginally high.

The brief descriptions below give a general idea of what it means to be high in any of the DiSC® dimensions, although your score can vary from somewhat high to very high.

D = Dominance

Here are typical behaviours you deploy to get things done if you score high in the Dominance dimension: you are driven, task-focused, assertive, and you can be forceful and aggressive depending on how high you are on the scale. You are motivated by power, authority and control, and one of your biggest fears is failure. If you score low in this trait, then you are likely to be mild, gentle, unassertive, possibly meek and non-confrontational.

I = Influence

If you score high in Influence, then these are typical behaviours you deploy to get things done: you are extroverted, a people person, gregarious, friendly and persuasive. You are motivated by the recognition from the endorsement of others, you draw energy from others. One of your biggest fears is rejection. If you score low in this trait you are reserved, introverted, retiring and self-motivated. In Myers-Briggs term, this is close to the Introversion-Extraversion dichotomy.

S = Steadiness

Here are typical behaviours you deploy to get things done if you score high in Steadiness: you are are dependable, reliable, consistent, evenly paced, kind and a safe pair of hands, a completer-finisher. You like the world around you being known and knowable and you are motivated by the security that creates. Your biggest fears are insecurity, turmoil and change. If you score low in this trait you are active, restless, impulsive, perhaps at the extreme – a headless chicken!

C = Compliance

If you are high on compliance, then here are typical behaviours that you deploy to get things done: you are careful, meticulous, precise and detailed. You like clear processes and like them to be followed. You are one of life's referees. The game must be played within the lines of the pitch and strictly to the rules. You are motivated by structure and good order and one of your biggest fears is chaos and conflict. If you score low in this trait you are likely to be a maverick, creative, unconventional, stubborn and non-conformist.

How does your dominant trait affect your speaking style?

We all display a mix of all four of these behavioural styles and we are certainly capable of choosing any of these styles on occasion. The purpose of any of these models, however, is to develop our self-awareness and enable us to identify our default modes.

Which are your dominant styles? Which one do you think is most like you? Which one do you think is your secondary style? In the following descriptions I'll use the Thomas International version of the DiSC® process.

If you want to know more and gain greater insight into your personality or behavioural style, almost all of these models are commercially available and can be taken as online tests in order to get an individual report. Many workplaces offer these as part of personal development.

If you are a high D

High D (Dominance) women are likely to be more confident to speak out. They are likely to be direct in their communication style and can be outspoken and forceful in how they articulate their views. If they see speeches and presentations as a means to an end, they will embrace them. They are unlikely to agonise about speaking up in meetings but will jump right in to ask questions and make their points. They will be forceful in ensuring they are heard; they will probably not allow themselves to be interrupted, or at the very least will ensure they come back to their point.

However, their direct and forceful style is most likely to cause issues *with likeability*. Their assertiveness will be perceived by some as aggression. Their outspokenness as unfeminine and therefore they will fall foul of the unconscious bias and may well be judged as not likeable.

When the high D traits in a woman are counterbalanced with high I or high S traits (eg kindness and focus on people), the impact of the High D directness is be softened and the speaker is therefore likely to gain wider acceptance and to experience less rejection as a result of likeability issues.

High D women are task- and achievement-focused and typically fear failure. This behavioural trait, when exacerbated by the *princess principle*, can put women under immense internal pressure and cause excess anxiety around some of the bigger speaking events.

If you are a high I

Given that women have already been socialised to be empathic, caring and concerned for others, high I (Influence) women, for whom external endorsement by others is important, feel the need to be people pleasers even more intensely. It makes them more worried about offending others if they speak up and therefore more inclined to self-edit and be cautious about how they speak (links to the *princess principle* and *cultural context*).

Since people who score high in the I dimension also need to be liked, high I women feel the fear of not being liked more intensely and may not want to run the risk of incurring criticism (*links to the critic and the Troll*), which equates with disapproval and rejection by others. This could mean that even though they are socially extroverted, on a professional level they could actively tone down how they speak, so as to not appear too assertive, too clever or too controversial.

In order to feel comfortable speaking out, high I, naturally extrovert women need their I traits to be counterbalanced with enough high D (Dominance) traits to prevent them from being held back by the need to be liked.

If you are low I

Low I (Influence) women are likely to be natural introverts, probably quieter and more shy than others. They typically hate being in the limelight and the whole idea of making a presentation or speech that puts them front and centre of attention is likely to be anathema to them. Even speaking up in a large meeting is likely to make them feel uncomfortable.

The natural performance anxiety that everyone experiences is felt even more intensely by low I women and exacerbated by the fear of incurring public criticism and judgment which, we have established, women know they will receive more than men. Low I women are therefore likely to be more susceptible to all the cultural pressures that silence women.

However, a woman with low I coupled with high D would not care so much about the judgment of others. The fact they are internally motivated and do not need the approval of others might make them more willing and able speak up and to challenge.

If you are high S

High S (Steadiness) women like stability and consistency and really want to fit in, not stand out. They are particularly attuned to societal norms and conventions and so it is likely that they will have a high tolerance for the status quo even if it is not ideal for them. They are unlikely to feel comfortable speaking up if it 'rocks the boat' or challenges convention in any way (*links to the 4,000-year silence project and cultural context*). Amiability and kindness are also high S traits, so high S women are likely to feel really uncomfortable with conflict and to keep quiet or heavily self-edit in order to avoid it. They are unlikely to be keen on many of the challenge tactics and options I've outlined in this book.

If you are high C

High C (Compliance) women like things to be accurate and precise. This means they are particularly prone to be perfectionists. Given the pressure on women to be perfect anyway (*link to the princess principle*), this can intensify the need to be perfect, to score 100% on all life's tests. As a result, high C women do not speak until and unless they have all the facts, the details and proof. They do not want to speak out in a meeting or volunteer to do a presentation unless they feel they are experts on the topic, fully prepared and have all the supporting data and information to hand. This often means they end up not speaking at all because the moment has passed by the time they have everything perfectly prepared. High C women may also increase their anxiety level by working all night, for example to (over) prepare for a presentation the next day.

They are also more likely to have a fixed mindset and see things as binary, right or wrong, good or bad, or accurate or inaccurate. This makes them unwilling to take risks and speak up because 'they are not good at it'. This is self-fulfilling. They never take the risk of giving a speech or presentation, which means they can never improve and develop skills. They rarely contribute in meetings because they do not want to risk not being right, so they never get to practise meeting interventions.

Finally, high C women are particularly at risk of suffering badly from *imposter syndrome* because rarely is anything perfect in real life. If you take an inherent need to be perfect from your behavioural style, add it to your societal conditioning as a female to be a perfect princess, you potentially have a perfect storm of perfectionism. Feeling like a constant failure to living up to that impossible standard can create massive imposter feelings, which can lead to never feeling you have a right to speak or be heard because you're not skilled or expert enough.

Self-awareness

Understanding how your behavioural style interacts with your willingness and ability to speak in public is helpful. If you typically really dislike giving presentations or speeches (beyond saying 'I just don't like them'), this can explain why.

For example, if you are a high S you are more likely to be inhibited by the societal norms and pressures like the need to be perfect and to be approved of. If you recognise the factors that have been affecting you, you then choose whether to allow them to continue doing so.

If you've always felt fine about speaking yet often feel like you struggle to be heard and be listened to, maybe it's because you're a high D and you communicate very directly, which can create resistance to your message.

The important point here is *never* that you should try to change who you are – it is to raise your awareness of your speaking and communication styles, and how they can come across and are received in your professional environment. This will help you develop style flexibility and enable you to speak and be heard better.

Most people always speak in their default mode, but the best speakers and communicators are able to adapt to their audiences. Speaking style flexibility is simply the ability to consciously adapt to situations in order to be more successful and advocate your ideas, proposals, and beliefs most effectively.

What to do

Know your own speaking style

Many millennials have thought about their personal brand, many have their own personal website to promote themselves, their careers or their business – perhaps you have too? Have you ever thought about your personal brand of speaking? The way we speak is buried in our hard wiring and determined by a mixture of our personality, level of confidence and competence, experiences, fears, socialisation and those all-pervasive societal paradigms.

By understanding where your 'default' style comes from you can consciously leverage your strengths and address areas of weakness. It can help you overcome the need to be perfect (and the fear of not being so) and choose and develop your own style.

What is your speaking style? For example, are you:

- emotional or logical?

- big picture or detail-oriented?

- structured or flexible / free flowing?

- empathic or detached?

- cool or warm?

- energetic or measured?

- direct or subtle?

- fast or slow?

- creative or factual?

- loud or quiet?

- proactive or reactive?

Step 1: define your style

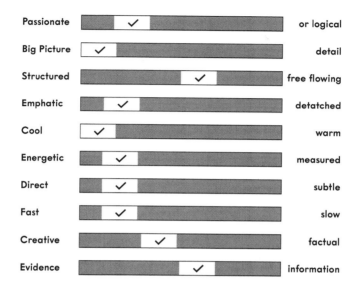

Passionate	✓	or logical
Big Picture	✓	detail
Structured	✓	free flowing
Emphatic	✓	detatched
Cool	✓	warm
Energetic	✓	measured
Direct	✓	subtle
Fast	✓	slow
Creative	✓	factual
Evidence	✓	information

The first step is to define your own default style. What do you typically do or like to do when speaking? A good way to do this is to self-assess and then ask friends and colleagues to also assess you, as we do not always perceive ourselves the same way as others do. To get a really accurate picture of your current style, you need to triangulate your perception with others.

Step 2: assess your speaking style

Next, ask yourself if that is a style you are comfortable with. Does it serve you well? Does it achieve your goals of being able to articulate your point of view and being heard? Or do you recognise some aspects of how you speak are the result of bending to societal norms or a subconscious reaction to criticisms you've had in the past? Are some aspects of your speaking style shaped by fear and anxiety?

Step 3: make any useful adjustments

That analysis will enable you to determine whether you want to make changes in any of these areas to find and develop your authentic 'voice', your speaking style. You may choose, for example, to lay down the need to be perfect, structured and prepared before you speak, which will enable you to speak out more in meetings. If your style is fast and direct and causing you to get caught in likability bias, then maybe you can choose to slow down and increase the subtlety factor in your style. The aim here is NOT to create a perfect style, just YOUR style.

Step 4: develop style flexibility

Once you are clear on your style, you can use the same analysis to determine whether it needs to be adapted for a particular audience. For instance, if your style is usually warm, empathic and free flowing but you're about to speak to a group of senior merchant bankers, you may want to adopt a more cool, detached and structured style for that particular audience.

Alternatively, you may choose not to adapt. You might want to use shock tactics and create an impact by deploying your style that is very different from what they are used to or typically like. The key point is that you will have made a conscious decision and not run into any issues unwittingly.

This process of combining your knowledge of the societal context, speaking skills and your own behavioural style will enable you to feel more comfortable speaking out in public and to have your voice heard.

Notes

You can use this space to make notes on any particular aspects of Part 2 that you think are relevant to you and you want to work on.

PART 3

APPLICATION/ ACTION

This final section brings together all of the skills and techniques outlined in the previous chapters into a useable checklist format to help you take action and apply those concepts.

CHAPTER 11

Meetings

Meetings are the crucible of business. They are often the source of key moments of debate and decision making. They are a forum for presenting your ideas, beliefs and opinions to a wide audience. Ideally, they are a platform for collaboration over ideas. As such, they are an opportunity for individuals to gain visibility, create reputations and build careers. They are an important forum for speaking effectively in public.

Too often, however, women find meetings challenging. Seema Kennedy, former MP, minister and Private Secretary to Theresa May, expressed a view that was common to many of the women I interviewed. She said: 'Sometimes meetings are much more petrifying than speeches.'

They can be a boisterous, combative environment and are sometimes used more for grandstanding and point scoring than achieving anything. Meetings don't always favour women's communication style, which is often more collaborative.

Many of my senior women interviewees preferred speaking events over meetings. They felt that with a presentation they had control and an audience who were obliged to listen, or at least appear to! Meetings, on the other hand, are often 'bunfights' in which it is much harder to be fully heard.

Women are often interrupted, shouted down or spoken over in meetings. As we established in Chapter 5, the fear of censure, criticism or just being ignored can cause women to refrain from speaking up. Often, women do intend to speak up but their 'perfection drivers' make them feel they can only speak if they have a killer point to make, are in possession of all the supporting facts and have it all mapped out.

One woman I interviewed, a Marketing Director in the pharmaceutical industry, said: 'I'll often wait until I've fully formulated what I want to say, I feel it has to be amazing before I speak.' The risk is that by the time you have everything prepared in your mind, the moment has gone and the discussion has moved on.

Some women report feeling intimidated and some say they simply do not see forcing their way into the fray as a productive use of time. Either way, this often causes women to consciously or subconsciously say less in meetings, to effectively be silenced.

And yet, meetings are important, so you should never allow yourself to be consciously or unconsciously silenced.

You must be well prepared for meetings and approach them strategically. This is true of men and women, but is perhaps more important for millennial women. When you are in the relatively early stages of your career, it is important to master meetings and harness their positive powers for effectiveness, recognition and advancement. The more challenging you find them, the more you should work to master them in the early years of your career.

10 steps for speaking and being heard in meetings

These top 10 points should be things you think about and prepare for going into every meeting. They come from my own experience in business, politics and working with clients, as well as interviews I have conducted with an array of senior women across all industries and business types.

1. Know the protocol

How does this meeting format work? Is it formal or informal? Is there a chair? If there is, get there early and introduce yourself to (or reacquaint yourself with) the chair, it may boost your chances of being invited to speak in the meeting and help enlist their help in ensuring you are not interrupted or spoken over. It may be that you send an email to the chair before the meeting to flag up your desire to speak or get your item on the agenda.

2. Agenda

Get your point on the agenda and ideally high up in the running order – you don't want your agenda item to be the one that gets bumped off when time runs out at the end. Martine Croxall (BBC news presenter and NUJ representative for the BBC women's group) recommends that you always make it your business to know all the items that are up for discussion and pick the ones you plan to contribute to. Knowing what you will contribute to in advance makes it much easier to speak up. If you wait to decide in the moment, it may be that you will never feel quite prepared enough and so will procrastinate and end up not saying anything. You should prepare your points and sometimes it's even worth rehearsing. Another interviewee, an executive head of a group of secondary schools said: 'To be taken seriously as a woman, you have to be more prepared, you can't wing it.'

3. Attendees

Do a bit of homework on the attendees. Knowing who they are and something about them (thank you, LinkedIn!) allows you to network with them and build rapport, especially with people you think are less inclined to support your views. People are less like likely to shout you down if you have engaged with them just before the meeting and they see you as a person, not an impersonal title. Find out who supports your views and who does not, that way you are less likely to be blindsided by unforeseen opposition to your ideas or points of view. Seema Kennedy's grandmother's advice to her was to 'stroke the bad dogs, the good ones won't bite you.'

4. Take up space

Don't sit at the edges and corners of the room. Take Sheryl Sandberg's advice and sit at the table and 'lean in'. Spread your files out and look like you belong there! Seema Kennedy (former MP) said that meetings often have more people than seats at the table, and that if you're junior or anxious, or both, it can feel more comfortable to sit at the edges, but you never should, it will only make it harder to be heard. Communicate confidence and status with your body language. That will influence people to take what you have to say seriously.

5. Less is more

You don't need to be talking all the time. Another interviewee, a senior engineer, says she follows the advice of a Finnish proverb: 'Only talk to improve upon the silence.' You can be pithy, punchy and precise, but you should always look to contribute something at every meeting you go to (otherwise why go?). One interviewee said she managed to get interrupted much less than other women because she was so punchy and to the point. If you view each meeting as an opportunity to build your career and credibility, then you must contribute and be visible.

6. Have a great point to make

By preparing well you can have the latest information, the best research, the up-to-date figures and be 'armed and dangerous' and ready to make a powerful, credible contribution. This is particularly important if you have strong perfection drivers. You absolutely do not need to be perfect, but being prepared will make you feel more comfortable. Given that women are often accorded less automatic credibility than men, being more prepared and ready to fully demonstrate your expertise is a useful tactic.

7. Speak early

Bigger meetings, perhaps with much more senior people, can be quite intimidating. One tactic is to ensure you plan to contribute early (if you can). Another woman I spoke with, the principal of a large further education college, said that earlier in her career, when she was more junior and more anxious, she found that speaking early gets that initial anxiety out of the way. You will then have contributed and probably feel more relaxed to contribute again.

8. Speak powerfully

When you choose to speak up, do it assertively. Speak with sufficient volume for the size of the room and the number of people in it. That will probably mean having to speak louder than you normally would. Get mentally prepared to do this. Don't use qualifiers or minimisers ('kinda', 'sort of', 'a bit', 'perhaps'), speak directly and unequivocally. Avoid 'uptalk' – you want to sound compelling, not like you're asking a question or seeking permission to make your point.

9. Use allies

Speak to people ahead of a meeting to get them to support you in the meeting. Agree that if you get interrupted or spoken over, or if your ideas are appropriated (Miss Triggs again!), you will each 'amplify' the other: 'I think X had an interesting perspective there, but I don't think she'd finished her point', or 'I agree with you, Tom, that's a good restatement of / build on the point Seema made, glad you agree with her.' Maybe a group of you can agree to do this for each other regularly in meetings.

Carrie Gracie, Martine Croxall and members of the BBC women's group that fought (and is still fighting) for equal pay at the BBC made a conscious agreement to do this for each other. Male colleagues can help too. This does not imply you are weak and need support, it is about subtly challenging culture by raising awareness of silencing behaviours that are not conducive to hearing all the ideas in any group.

10. Deal with interruptions

Develop some lines you feel comfortable with to insist you be allowed to finish your point if you get interrupted. The college principal mentioned above said that earlier in her career, she would feel silenced and would just take it until she got so frustrated she would blurt out an angry response, which ultimately did not do much to help her be heard. So, she developed better strategies for dealing with interruptions. Better to be prepared with a favourite phrase like: 'Hold on a minute, I haven't quite finished', or 'Let me finish the point' or 'Could you let me finish and we can then come to your point?'

Another interviewee, a general counsel and board member of a FinTech business, uses the phrase: 'You need to let me finish', using a calm tone and a slight downward intonation of command. She finds this gets the right response from anyone who interrupts her. The specific phraseology has to be congruent with your style and can be direct, but it is better not to be rude or confrontational, not because you should be a 'good girl' but because that will leave someone simmering with anger at you, and therefore unlikely to be listening much to what you have to say!

Digital meetings

How does this apply to digital platform-based meetings and presentations? It is worth mentioning here some specific tips for meetings that take place remotely via web conference or video conferencing platforms.

Being heard in a Zoom meeting of 10, 20, 30 or more people can be really challenging. Without body language cues, people's propensity to interrupt each other can be even greater than in face-to-face situations. For women to speak in big digital meetings can require even more assertive behaviours. However, if people interrupt and speak over others on these digital platforms, the effect is that no one can be heard.

In some respects, this seems to have resulted in digital meetings having greater structure and more process or protocols around speaker selection and how meeting interventions are to be made, such as hand raising via actual hands or digital icons. Many feel this has favoured women and made it easier for them to contribute.

It means that there is a greater responsibility on the chair of a digital meeting. To be effective, they need to:

- proactively invite comments from a cross-section of people rather than allow an inaudible free for all

- prepare more and be even more alert to fairness and the need to invite a representative cross-section of views

- encourage the use of chat box functionality as a fair way to ensure everyone has an equal opportunity to contribute and ask questions

If these protocols or processes are not in place in the digital meetings you attend, then you should consider speaking to the chair to suggest introducing them to create more productive meetings for all.

CHAPTER 12

Presentations and Speeches

Speech is power: speech is to persuade,
to convert, to compel.

Ralph Waldo Emerson

To summarise, presentations and speeches are disproportionately important to your career, reputation and influence. They are your showroom. They are the opportunity to articulate and showcase your ideas, your solutions and your beliefs to much wider audiences. They can define your role, your reputation, and your career.

Almost all senior roles in business, whether in the public sector or politics, require you to present and speak. And yet, presentations and speeches are also the point of maximum exposure. They are a performance, with all the attendant risks and performance anxiety. As I have established throughout the book, these risks and anxieties are often heightened by societal pressure on women.

Here are 10 things to think about when giving speeches or presentations that you can use as a checklist when preparing for a speaking event.

Preparation

1. Make time to prepare

It takes a lot of preparation to deliver a good speech or presentation, and even more to make it seem informal, conversational and spontaneous. Many of the women I interviewed said it has only become really clear to them relatively recently that the best speakers, who seem to be 'just naturals', are in fact those who put the most time into preparation. Many of these senior women are incredibly busy and do not much like the conclusion they have reached, but nonetheless, they are now very clear about the fact that speaking well requires plenty of preparation time.

I always recommend to my clients that they assess each speech or presentation they do on a sliding scale of importance, with 1 being a routine, small, in-house presentation with people who already know you well and 10 being your biggest 'gig' of the year – for example an industry event, a kick-off meeting for the whole team, a whole-company meeting, a selection or interview presentation for your dream role.

Once you have a clear idea of where this particular speaking event sits on that scale, allocate the commensurate amount of time to preparation. You also need to recognise that 'the commensurate amount of time' is probably more than you think it is!

2. Audience analysis

You must know and research your audience. A good presentation is not about what you want to tell people, it is about what they want to hear. For you to engage them you must know where they are coming from. For you to influence them and bring them with you, you must know them well enough to know what *they* need to hear in order for *you* to achieve your objective. What do they need to hear to buy into your ideas, your proposal, your beliefs?

Faced with the likability double bind (the risk of being disliked if you come across as powerful), a good audience analysis will also help you decide on the style you need to adopt to be in synch with this audience and give yourself the best chance of being heard and convincing them.

3. Rehearse

I've established that many millennial women are plagued by imposter syndrome and worry about unfair criticism, which can damage confidence. One way to address this is to make time to rehearse − and by rehearsing, I mean speaking out loud.

I spoke with a communications director based in Hong Kong who said: 'There's a world of difference from just going through your talking points compared to speaking them out loud.' Often, what reads well on the page does not work as well when spoken, and if you do not rehearse, you won't know that until you're stumbling through words in front of your audience!

By rehearsing well, you build confidence and competence which enables you to use facts and your sense of preparedness to dispel your emotional (irrational but real) anxiety. This is not about being perfect (more about being brave) − I rarely recommend that clients script and learn a speech word for word, even for the biggest gigs (unless you're using an autocue). It is more about rehearsing, at first using a full script to get comfortable with the words and phrases, and then condensing it to bullet points. Once you know what to say and the words and phrases are in your mind, the bullet points are enough to remind you. You do not normally have to be word perfect, in fact you often sound more authentic when you are not.

Even for speaking events you consider to be of lower importance, make time to rehearse the beginning and the end. Since that is mostly what people remember anyway, being confident and prepared at the beginning and end and getting off to a good start means you will get away with a multitude of sins in the middle!

Delivery

4. Own the space

If you possibly can, arrive early at the venue where you are due to speak. Get into the meeting room, lecture theatre or auditorium and familiarise yourself with the layout and feel of the room. If you like to move about while speaking, nothing is worse than turning up to speak in a cramped meeting room when you're not ready for it.

Working out the layout beforehand gives you time to think through how you might adapt your style or plan according to the available space. If getting there early is not possible, you can often ask the event organisers for the layout of the room or the details of the venue.

From a psychological standpoint, voice coach Sally Bishop urges clients to walk, or at least look, around the room, noticing small details like carpet colour or pictures on the walls in order to make you feel grounded and comfortable in the space. Arriving early or first enables you to welcome people into the room and makes it, in some sense, your space, which is a more comfortable feeling than entering an alien environment. This can certainly help reduce any imposter syndrome-led anxiety.

5. Manage your state

When you stand up to speak, the pressures on you can be intense, especially if you are a younger female speaker. Concerns around criticism, failure, embarrassment, rejection or dismissal of you and your message can seriously impair your ability to get your message across and be heard. Learning techniques to manage your emotional state during and leading up to speaking events is an important skill.

The best advice? Breathe! Voice coach Sally Bishop tells clients to 'breathe like it's OK!' What she means is take deeper breaths, which aids your voice production (by putting oxygen in the tank) and, more importantly, calms your body down by telling it that it's not at risk of running out of oxygen.

The other key here is to manage your 'self-talk'. If you suffer from imposter syndrome (and 90% of the women I interviewed said they do, or did) and you let it, it will go into overdrive in the moments of nervousness leading up to, and sometime during, a speaking event. You need to control the internal dialogue and instead of saying to yourself 'they're going to hate me, I'm out of my depth, they'll know I'm a fraud', you need to make a conscious decision to tell those negative voices to shut up and replace them with a soundtrack of more positive thoughts: 'I know my stuff, I've worked hard, I have an expert and credible view to share, I deserve to be here'.

You are in control of your own thought processes. This is called metacognition, meaning thinking about thinking. Think about how some of the societal norms and unconscious biases have influenced your thinking and caused you to have negative and disempowering thoughts surrounding speaking and being heard. Make a conscious choice to replace those thoughts with more empowering ones that encourage and enable you.

6. Make use of emotion

Emotional intelligence is typically a female asset. Understanding where an audience is emotionally on the topic you are about to speak on is useful. Are they happy, sad, frustrated, angry, disengaged or bored? This enables you to work with and use those emotions.

Using a full range of rhetorical devices to engage your audience's emotions is a way to persuade and bring them with you. Telling stories, using allegorical tales, using metaphors, framing the debate in terms of protagonist and antagonist – all of these are powerful tools to elicit a positive emotional response from an audience without necessarily using emotive language that risks criticism.

7. Assertive body language

Manage your body language to exude confidence and status. Women who speak very forcefully often fall foul of the likeability double bind (where they are criticised because they project as too 'strident', 'unfeminine' or simply not 'likeable'. One way around that is to use your body language to convey power, status and credibility.

Body language is read by others mostly subconsciously, but it is a powerful part of how your message comes across. A balanced, strong stance, expansive gestures, keeping your head up and making good eye contact with your audience all convey the message that this person has confidence and authority. Without saying a word, you tell the audience that here is a person of status and credibility, someone to whom I should listen.

If you also speak in a voice that is firm and loud enough to have presence, with a tone and language that are positive and assured, you create a powerful presence.

8. Structure

Start and end presentations and speeches strongly. A beginning like 'Hello, my name is… and I'm here to speak about…' is OK but frankly dull (and often that's what is on the slide behind you, so it's also somewhat redundant).

It is better to start a speech with something impactful, a big number, a joke, a surprising statistic, a good quote. Start with something that is a bit different and grabs the audience's attention. If you can get them to engage with you early and you start getting good feedback from them, it will settle and encourage you.

Similarly, finish with a bang and not a whimper! Always have your final sentence or two well prepared so you can leave the audience with something memorable. It could be something like 'I leave you with this final thought' or 'If you take away only one thing from my talk today, remember this…'

Question response structure

When it comes to the Q&A section of a presentation or speech, knowing and using a brief structure can be really helpful in giving you a quick way to organise your thoughts when answering questions (this works in meetings as well).

For example, the 3Ps: *Point, Proof, Punchline* – deliver your key point, deliver some data or evidence and summarise your point with a pithy sentence, ideally a memorable one.

The 3Ss, *Situation, Solution, Steps,* are a good structure for problem-solving comments. First, you outline the situation or context and background – what is the problem or opportunity? Next, what is the answer to the problem – the solution? Finally, how do you grasp the opportunity, what do you do about it and what is the call to action – what are the next steps?

Using these enables you to structure your ideas quickly, even if you only have a minute to gather your thoughts.

9. Diffusing hostility, frustration or anger

Being faced with questioners who are angry or hostile can be a particularly challenging scenario, whether a political hustings or a presentation where you have had to announce redundancies or an unpopular policy, for example.

Handling a hostile questioner requires you to roll with the punches. Essentially, your instinctive response might be to counterattack. It is best not to do that, as it usually only adds heat to the flames – and if you are a younger woman being questioned by an older man who potentially still works on the 4,000-year silence paradigm, that inflammation will be all the greater.

Instead, listen to what is being said and acknowledge the speaker's feelings or emotion: 'I can see this means a lot to you / is upsetting for you' or 'I can understand that you feel angry about this.' You can restate their point, eg: 'I can see that these redundancies are far from ideal.'

Making someone feel heard is usually a way to diffuse their anger, whereas immediately dismissing or invalidating their point of view can inflame emotions. The key point here is you don't have to agree with them, just reflect and acknowledge what they've said.

Showing empathy is good, you can demonstrate understanding and it is not the same as sympathy which is essentially agreement or shared feeling. This should hopefully 'draw the sting' from the situation and lay a good foundation for you to segue to the point you want to make. However, be sure not to use the word 'but', as this tends to invalidate anything you've said before to calm them down!

10. Time to think

There will always be times when you are asked a question to which you do not immediately know the answer. The first thing to do is ask for more information from the questioner to ensure you have fully understood their question. Feeling that you don't know the answer is often a function of a poor question!

Don't let your 'imposter' automatically tell you that you're the problem, it could be the questioner! Don't let your perfection drivers tell you that you 'ought' to know all the answers either, because a) nobody does and b) telling yourself that makes you feel bad and therefore puts you in a less psychologically resourceful state to handle the question.

You could use phrases like 'Could you expand on that for me?', 'Not sure I've fully understood the question, could you say a little more?' or 'There seem to be a few questions tied up in what you asked there, could you separate them for me so I can be sure to capture them all?' As well as giving you more information, this buys you more time to process the question and formulate a response.

It is also OK to say that you don't know. On the whole, women are more comfortable with humility and admitting they do not know the answer. The key thing is to promise to get back to the questioner with a response and ensure you do so!

Notes

Capture your thoughts here on how and when you can put into practice whichever parts are most relevant to you.

Knowing is not enough; we must apply.
Willing is not enough; we must do.

Goethe, *Wilhelm Meister's Apprenticeship*

Conclusion

Standing on the shoulders of giants

Generations of women have fought the battles for equality that have given millennial women the opportunities they have today: the right to vote, the right to work, the right not to be actively discriminated against on the basis of sex, the right to equal pay, the right to control our own bodies, all of these have required significant battles.

In the western world legislation is in place that enshrines these rights in law. In many respects, millennial women could be forgiven for thinking that equality is fully realised and they have an entirely level playing field on which to build their lives and careers.

However, as I've demonstrated in this book, speaking out and being heard is still not easy for women, especially women of colour. Many centuries-old societal paradigms (and some new digital manifestations that are perpetuating them) still govern the way women are perceived and limit their ability to be really heard. The playing field is far from level. This limits the ability of individual women to progress into senior leadership roles and change the processes and structures that need to change to achieve full equality.

The issue is that the problems and barriers women face in being heard are much more subtle and therefore more insidious than they were back in the 1960s and 1970s and earlier times. They are like rocks beneath the surface. When you look ahead, the sea looks flat, calm, inviting even. It looks like plain sailing. Only it is not.

The subtle pressures and barriers of the imposter syndrome, the various forms of unconscious bias, the silencing effect of criticism and microaggressions, all of these are sharp rocks beneath the surface, waiting for you and your career to run aground on. You may not even notice any of these 'rocks' early on in your career, but they tend to become more and more of an issue the more senior you get.

The ability to speak out and to be heard is the gateway to successful careers, which in turn are the gateway to social change and equality. When women are discouraged from speaking up, when their ideas and their views are not heard, then individuals and society lose potentially half the good ideas of all humanity! When half of humanity feels unheard and under-represented, it is neither effective nor fair.

This book is about what individual women themselves can do to speak up and be heard. It's about you becoming more comfortable and confident in articulating your thoughts, ideas and views. It is about lessening your anxiety, advancing your professional success and increasing your circle of influence.

Whether you want to do that for your individual benefit or to tackle the issues of gender inequality is up to you, but both are inextricably linked. I hope the 'what to do' tactics will prove to be practical suggestions for you to deploy, whether you choose to challenge the system or navigate it.

Challenging or navigating is always an individual choice based on the particular context, your circumstances and your objectives. It may well be that you navigate earlier in your career while you build your expertise, knowledge and reputation. Once more established and more senior, you are probably better placed to challenge and make a bigger impact.

If you do choose to challenge, the advice from Carrie Gracie and Martine Croxall would be to not do it alone. Find your tribe and work at it together.

Get involved in the conversation and share your challenges and success at www.patriciaseabright.com and www.archimedesspeaks.com

But whatever route you take and whatever you do, Speak Up, Speak Out and Be Heard!

Resources

Websites

- arementalkingtoomuch.com

- fawcettsociety.org.uk

- Fixtheglitch.org

- Leanin.org

- speakingwhilefemale.co

- www.thefemalelead.com

- TED Talk – Brave Not Perfect:
  https://www.youtube.com/watch?v=fC9da6eqaqg

- TED Talk – Why We Have Too Few Women Leaders:
  https://www.youtube.com/watch?v=fC9da6eqaqg

Additional reading

- Beard, M., *Women & Power: A Manifesto,* 2017

- *Cameron, D., The myth of Mars and Venus: Do Men and Women Really Speak Different Languages?*

- Chamorro-Premuzic, T., *Why Do So Many Incompetent Men Become Leaders?*

- Clinton, H., *What Happened*

- Cooper, Y., *She Speaks: The Power of Women's Voices*

- Covey, S. R., *Habits of Effective Managers*

- Covey, S. R., *The 7 Habits of Highly Effective People*, 1999

- Criado-Perez, C., *Invisible Women*

- Davidson, R., *Yes She Can*

- Dweck, C., *Mindset*

- Goyder, C., *Gravitas: Communicate with Confidence, Influence and Authority*

- Gracie, C., *Equal*

- Holland, J., *A Brief History of Misogyny: The World's Oldest Prejudice (Brief Histories)*

- Lancaster, S., *Speechwriting: the Expert Guide*

- Lewis, H., *Difficult Women: An Imperfect History of Feminism*

- Morrisey, H., *A Good Time to be a Girl*

- Obama, M., *Becoming*

- Rodenburg, P., *The Right to Speak: Working with the Voice*

- Sandbery, S., *Lean In: Women, Work and the Will to Lead*

- Saujani, R., *Brave not Perfect*, 2019

Endnotes

Chapter 1

1   Nancy C., Silva, C., *The Myth of the Ideal Worker*, 2011

https://www.catalyst.org/wp-content/uploads/2019/02/The_Myth_of_the_Ideal_Worker_Does_Doing_All_the_Right_Things_Really_Get_Women_Ahead.pdf

2   Giddon, A., Quoted by Naomi Wold, Article in *The Guardian*, 24 July 2015

3   Influence of Communication Partner's Gender on Language, Hancock, A. B., Rubin, B. A., First Published 11 May 2014, Research Article

https://doi.org/10.1177/0261927X14533197

4   Duncan, R. (1998) 'Miss Triggs' [Cartoon], *Punch*

5   Gracie, C., *Equal*, 2019

6   House of Commons Library 'How much less were women paid in 2019?' Published Monday, 6 January 2020, Brigid Francis-Devine

https://commonslibrary.parliament.uk/economy-business/economy-economy/how-much-less-were-women-paid-in-2019

7   Watson, C., Uberoi, E., & Kirk-Wade, E., 'Women in Parliament and Government' Published Tuesday, 25 February 2020

This briefing includes latest figures on the proportion of women in parliament and elected bodies across the UK and throughout the world.

https://commonslibrary.parliament.uk/research-briefings/sn01250/

8   https://cawp.rutgers.edu/women-us-congress-2020

9   https://www.fawcettsociety.org.uk/news/new-fawcett-data-reveals-that-womens-representation-in-local-government-at-a-standstill

10   BEIS press release, February 2020

https://www.gov.uk/government/news/third-of-ftse-100-board-members-now-women-but-business-secretary-says-more-needs-to-be-done

Catalyst.org research published 13/3/20

https://www.catalyst.org/research/women-on-corporate-boards/

11   Kings College London research article published 14 January 2020

https://www.kcl.ac.uk/news/womens-unpaid-care-work-has-been-unmeasured-and-undervalued-for-too-long

12   Criado-Perez, C., *Invisible Women*, 2019

13   Shaw, G.B., *Pygmalion*, 1913

Musical film, *My Fair Lady*, words and music Lerner, A. J. & Loewe, F., 1964

Chapter 2

14   Beard, M., *Women & Power: A Manifesto*, 2017

15   Purvis, J., Article in *The Guardian* 13 November 2007

16   Clinton, H., *What Happened*, 2017

17   Bizzabo, Gender Diversity & Inclusion in Events Report.

https://blog.bizzabo.com/event-gender-diversity-study-2019

18   Salvaire, A., e-book, *Balance the World*, 2018

https://www.amazon.co.uk/Balance-world-Tactics-launch-revolution/dp/198199100X

19   Article quoting a commission Harriet Harman MP set up; article in *The Guardian* by Jane Martinson, Wednesday 15 May 2013

https://www.theguardian.com/media/2013/may/15/female-tv-presenters-ageism-sexism

20   Study 'Sex Roles, Interruptions and Silences in Conversations' Zimmerman, D., & West, C., sociologists at the University of California, Santa Barbara, 1975

21   McKinsey Report, 2019, Wikipedia

22   Shaw, S., 'Governed by the rules, the female voice in Parliamentary debate', 1999

Also quoted in Deborah Cameron's book *The Myth of Mars and Venus*, 2007

23   Tweet from Jackie Speier

https://speier.house.gov/2020/1/democratic-womens-caucus-members-send-letter-to-president-trump-condemning-his-continuing-degradation-of-women

24   Sandberg, S., *Lean In: Women, Work and the Will to Lead*, 2013

Chapter 3

25   Bizzabo, Gender Diversity & Inclusion in Events Report.

https://blog.bizzabo.com/event-gender-diversity-study-2019

26   Saujani, R., *Brave not Perfect*, 2019

27   Mathews, G., 'Imposter phenomenon: attributions for success and failure', paper presented at the American Psychological Association, 1984

28   Carter, C. M., Article in Forbes, November 2016

https://www.forbes.com/sites/christinecarter/2016/11/01/why-so-many-millennials-experience-imposter-syndrome/#7765b5116aeb

29   Sandberg, S., *Lean In: Women, Work and the Will to Lead*, 2015

30   Dweck, C., *Mindset*, 2012

31   Jeffers, S., *Feel the Fear and Do it Anyway*, 1987

Chapter 4

32   Sandberg, S., *Lean In: Women, Work and the Will to Lead*, 2015

33   Cialdini, R., *Influence: the Psychology of Persuasion*, 1999

Chapter 5

34   https://www.amnesty.org.uk/online-violence-women-mps

35   https://fixtheglitch.org/2018/12/19/amnestys-latest-research-into-online-abuse-confirms-what-black-women-have-known-for-over-a-decade/

36   Occasio-Cortez, A., speech delivered in Congress, 23 July 2020, Reported by *The Guardian*

https://www.theguardian.com/us-news/2020/jul/23/aoc-speech-video-ted-yoho

37   Criado-Perez, C., *Invisible Women*, 2019

38   Brescoll, V., Dawson, E. & Uhlmann, E.L., 'Hard Won and Easily Lost: The Fragile Status of Leaders in Gender-Stereotype-Incongruent Occupations', 2016

https://gap.hks.harvard.edu/hard-won-and-easily-lost-fragile-status-leaders-gender-stereotype-incongruent-occupations

39   Amnesty International, Report: Toxic Twitter- a toxic place for women

https://www.amnesty.org/en/latest/research/2018/03/online-violence-against-women-chapter-1/

40   Goleman, D., *Emotional Intelligence*, 1997

Chapter 6

41   Lakoff, R., *Language and Woman's Place*, 1973

42   Gray, J., *Men Are from Mars, Women Are from Venus*, 1992

43   Cameron, D., *The Myth of Mars and Venus: Do Men and Women Really Speak Different Languages?*, 2007

44   https://www.telegraph.co.uk/politics/2020/05/11/wives-children-researchers-will-able-vote-laws-new-coronavirus/

Chapter 7

45   Mehrabian, A., *Silent Messages*, 1971

46   Wolf, N., 'Young women, give up the vocal fry and reclaim your strong female voice', *The Guardian*, 24 July 2015

https://www.theguardian.com/commentisfree/2015/jul/24/vocal-fry-strong-female-voice

47   Cameron, D., Blog, 26/7/ 2015

https://debuk.wordpress.com/2015/07/26/a-response-to-naomi-wolf/

48   Criado-Perez, C., *Invisible Women*, 2019

49   Article in Berkley News, October 2018

https://news.berkeley.edu/2018/10/09/podcast-sounding-american-gender-and-politics/

Chapter 8

50   Chamorro-Premuzic, T., *Why Do So Many Incompetent Men Become Leaders?*, 2019

51   Obama, M., *Becoming*, 2018

Chapter 9

52   Goleman, D., *Emotional Intelligence*, 1997

53   Salerno, J. M., & Peter-Hagene, L. C., 'One Angry Woman: Anger Expression Increases Influence for Men, but Decreases Influence for Women, During Group Deliberation', *Law and Human Behavior*, 2015 doi:10.1037/lhb0000147

54   Obama, M., *Becoming*, 2018

Chapter 10

55   Keirsey, D., *Please Understand ME: 2: Temperament, Character, Intelligence*, 1984

About the author

When Patricia was at school, she used to love participating in public speaking competitions. One topic she chose to speak on was the 300 Group, a group dedicated to achieving gender parity in the UK Parliament. Many years later she found herself increasingly frustrated that this still hasn't happened and that gender equality in all walks of life is still far from achieved.

Patricia has spent her career in the sales and marketing business and latterly in her own consultancy business, Archimedes Consulting Ltd. Her focus has always been sales, communication and influence. She has worked on public speaking coaching with a wide range of senior leaders in business and politics. One of her proudest achievements recently is to have coached the new female MP who was the first to deliver her maiden speech remotely during the COVID-19 pandemic.

She has worked with many very successful women, and yet the frustration is still there that in all professional arenas, public sector, business and politics, so many women do not achieve their full potential. Why is this? Why is progress towards gender equality so glacially slow?

As she reflected on this it became clear to her that one major barrier is women's struggle to speak in public and to be heard. So many of the brilliant women Patricia has worked with either find it hard to speak up in big meetings or/and dislike presentations or speeches, while those who are happy to speak up frequently say they don't feel heard.

Because Patricia feels passionately that a gender balanced world will be a better world, particularly as the proud mother of two girls, she decided to write this book to help women – especially millennial women – tackle some of the issues and barriers that prevent them from realising their full potential and being heard.

Patricia brings her years of experience and her unique and straightforward approach to this book which is packed with useful and actionable approaches.

Contact her and share your experiences at www.patriciaseabright.com and www.archimedesspeaks.com

Printed in Great Britain
by Amazon